Bars and Restaurants

Bars and Restaurants

Editor: Paco Asensio

Editorial coordination: Alejandro Bahamón and Aurora Cuito

Introduction: Alejandro Bahamón

Text: Alejandro Bahamón, Cristina Montes, Aurora Cuito

Translation: Julie King

Art direction: Mireia Casanovas Soley

Layout: Pilar Cano

Domènech, 7-9 2º 2ª. 08012 Barcelona. Spain
Tel.: +34 93 218 30 99
Fax: +34 93 237 00 60
loft@loftpublications.com
www.loftpublications.com

Softcover ISBN: 0-8230-0439-2
Hardcover ISBN: 0-06-621360-6

D.L.: B-47.370-01

First published in 2001 by LOFT and HBI,
an imprint of HarperCollins International
10 East 53rd St. New York, NY 10022-5299

Distributed in the U.S. and Canada by Watson-Guptill Publications
770 Broadway New York, NY 10003-9595
Telephone: (800) 451-1741 or (732) 363-4511 in NJ, AK, HI Fax: (732) 363-0338

Distributed throughout the rest of the world by
HarperCollins International
10 East 53rd St. New York, NY 10022-5299
Fax: (212) 207-7654

If you would like to suggest projects for inclusion in
our next volumes, please e-mail details to us at:
loft@loftpublications.com

Within the contemporary urban landscape and the wide variety of places that make up its complex fabric, interior spaces are becoming more valuable than exterior spaces. Because of climate, security, leisure time, and comfort, interiors are an important part of public activity and our urban lives. We go through airports, train stations, commercial centers, building lobbies, and galleries along our path through the city each day. However, the most intense personal exchange often takes place in a bar or restaurant. Most bars and restaurants are open to everyone and are a type of public space for activity and entertainment. Inside their walls, deals are closed, acquaintances are made, love is declared, and relationships are ended. They are a place for flirtation and camaraderie, for entertainment and relaxation, for seeing and being seen.

Over time, the interiors of bars and restaurants have required a unique style, and have moved beyond the impersonal look that defined them decades ago. For this reason, the role of architects and designers is fundamental to the design of their interiors. The layout, proportions, lighting, and type of furnishings selected for a bar or restaurant determine its mood, whether euphoric, rowdy, or intimate.

In the following pages, we have compiled a selection of bars and restaurants that stand out for their interior design.

The projects are provocative due to the range of sensations the settings produce. From the restless organic forms of the new restaurant at the Georges Pompidou Center to the most radical proposal of textures and colors created by Fabio Novembre for Shu, the book presents infinite interior design solutions and pays special attention to every detail and corner. Each project illustrates how materials are used and how decorative objects are presented.

The book is organized into three chapters that are related to the public and private character of each place. In general, bars are found in the first part of the book since they have a more active character and are often linked to the exterior. Restaurants are found in the latter part of the book, since they usually imply a more intimate and private ambience. In the middle are those projects that combine the two functions. The selection includes some of the most recognized design from bars and restaurants around the world. The examples submerge us in the design world and stimulate our senses. All the projects take us on a journey to a place where we can appreciate the trends and design solutions. They also reveal and bring us closer to the interior of these cities' hidden public spaces.

Bars

Norman Bar

JAM Design | **Leeds**

For decades, Leeds, a small city in the north of England, was overshadowed by Manchester, a booming industrial town that became famous in the 70´s and 80´s for its musical bars. However, in the years since, an old and desolate neighborhood in Leeds known as The Calls has experienced a resurgence. Known for its Victorian architecture, The Calls is now home to a string of clubs, restaurants, and bars that have sprung up in an effort to convert Leeds into the 24-hour capital of northern England. The restaurant-bar Norman, designed by the young firm, JAM, has one of the area's most surprising, creative interior designs.

The idea behind Norman, with a capacity for 80 seats, was to create a space that combines contemporary design with a warm and active atmosphere. To achieve this goal, the designers reached out to an entire team of collaborators. The philosophy was that each team would enrich the overall design by focusing on an individual project. Tom Dixon specially designed the furnishings for the space, Inflate orchestrated the lighting, Fly controlled the graphics, and Tracy Davidson contributed pieces of contemporary art.

Norman Bar combines a series of objects with lightly earthy forms, soft textures, bright colors, and an informal and fun atmosphere

A glance across the glass façade makes the visitor momentarily forget that Norman is a restaurant and not an exhibition space for contemporary furnishings. Fluffy sofas placed near the façade submerge those who recline on them. The mood is also set by low tables in tones of red, gray, and orange that seem like pieces of river rock cut in half. As a complement, Tom Dixon designed chairs out of luminous plastic that shine in the darkness. A television, suspended from an installation in the ceiling, further enriches the interior space.

Architect: JAM (Jamie Anley, Astrid Zala and Matthieu Paillard)

Collaborators: Tom Dixon (furnishings); Inflate (lighting); Fly (graphic design); Tracy Davidson (art)

Photographer: James Winspear/VIEW

Address: 36 Call Lane, Leeds, United Kingdom

Opening date: January 1998

Surface area: 1,935 sq. feet

◀
Tom Dixon also designed the bar stools, which are slightly taller than the rest of the chairs in the restaurant. They line up with the top of the bar, which is made out of yellow glass fibers, illuminated underneath to reflect light to the rest of the space.

The interior's dominating element is an enormous, undulating wall that crosses the entire area of the bar-restaurant. Made in a metal structure to which concrete has been applied, the wall separates the kitchen zone and marks off a more tranquil area from the rest of the space.

▼

Kosushi

Arthur de Mattos Casas | **São Paulo**

A large Japanese population settled in Sao Paulo, Brazil years ago. As a result, the Brazilian culture is often associated with Asian culinary tastes, and there is an extensive variety of restaurants that fuse the two worlds. Brazil's Modern Movement has also encouraged designers to create furnishings and decorative elements that respond to the Asian aesthetic. Thus, the main challenge in the design of this bar, located in the city center, was to emphasize this cultural symbiosis.

The bar Kosushi was conceived as the extension of a restaurant with the same name that has a recognized history in the city. The objective was to creative a space that alludes to Japanese design, but does not fall into the typical, traditional Asian style. To achieve this goal, the architect used a formal contemporary language, emphasizing materials like metal, polished stone, or glass, while incorporating decorative Asian touches like mats made out of bamboo and wood, or large panels depicting the grandfathers of sushi.

The mixture of materials, textures, and references to the Brazilian and Japanese cultures enriches this space, which is inspired by the furnishings from the 50's

The furnishings are Brazilian pieces from the 50´s that pay tribute to Japanese furniture from the same era. The interior distribution gives special importance to the patio, which is found in a corner of the establishment and is the element that articulates all the spaces. The patio divides the main room from a small private room and controls off the circulation and access. The resulting spatial richness is emphasized by the placement and diversity of the furnishings. Different ambiences are created within the same space.

Architect: Arthur de Mattos Casas

Collaborators: Gilberto Elkis (garden)

Photographer: Tuca Reins

Address: Arthur Ramos Street, São Paulo, Brazil

Opening date: April 1999

Surface area: 5,430 sq. feet

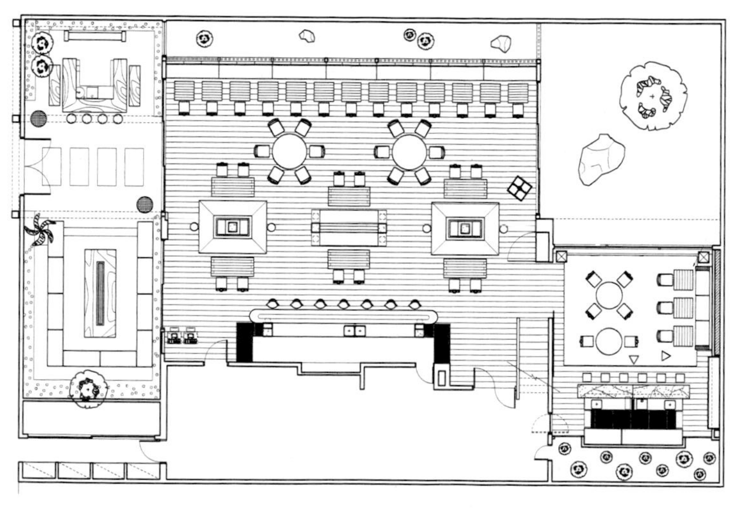

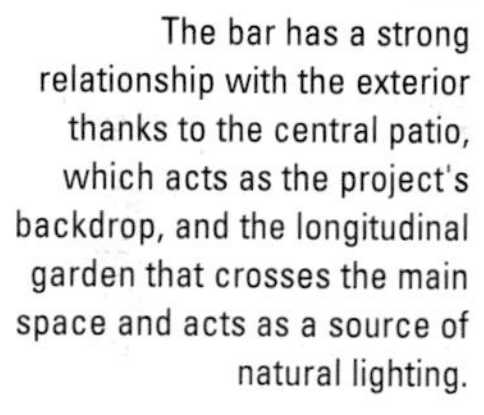

The bar has a strong relationship with the exterior thanks to the central patio, which acts as the project's backdrop, and the longitudinal garden that crosses the main space and acts as a source of natural lighting.

Diversity in the distribution and furnishings permits different situations within the same space, from bar stools the same height as the bar to comfortable sofas where visitors can relax.

▲

The interior's warm and tranquil atmosphere is achieved through a homogeneous palette of soft tones that range from brown to sand.

The service zone is noteworthy for its elemental geometric forms, indirect lighting across glass partitions, and minimalist objects.

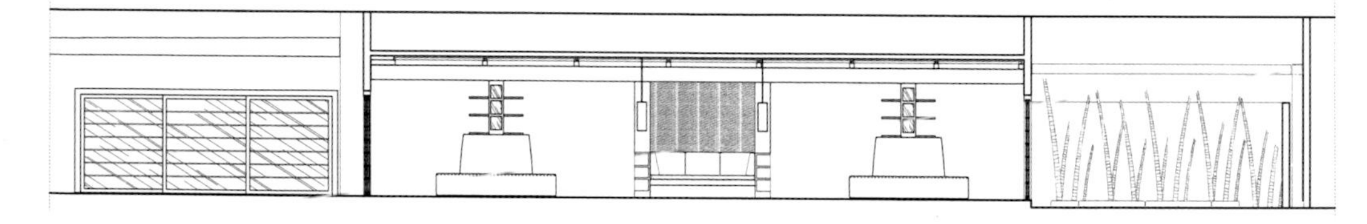

Longitudinal section

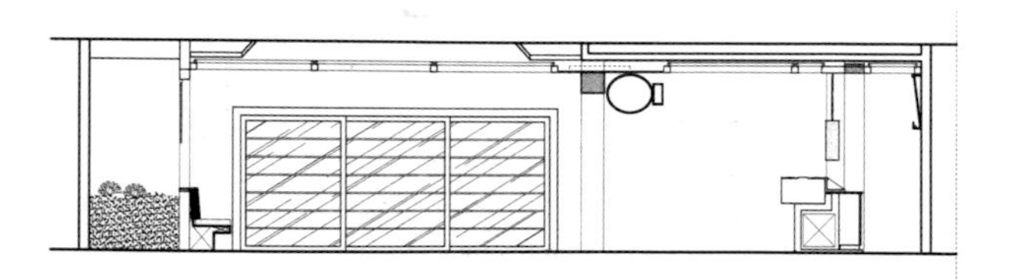

Transversal section

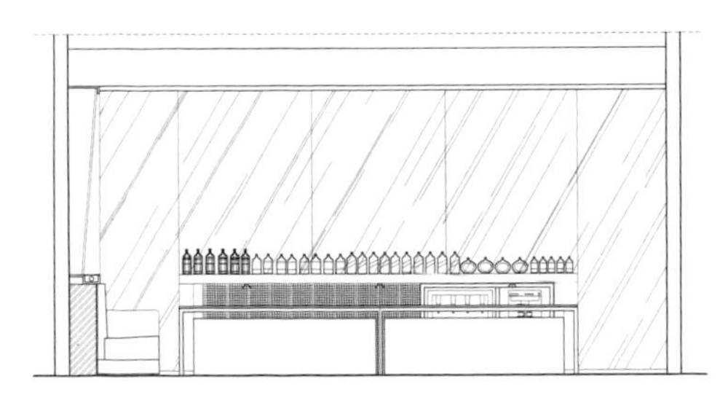

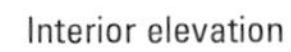

Interior elevation

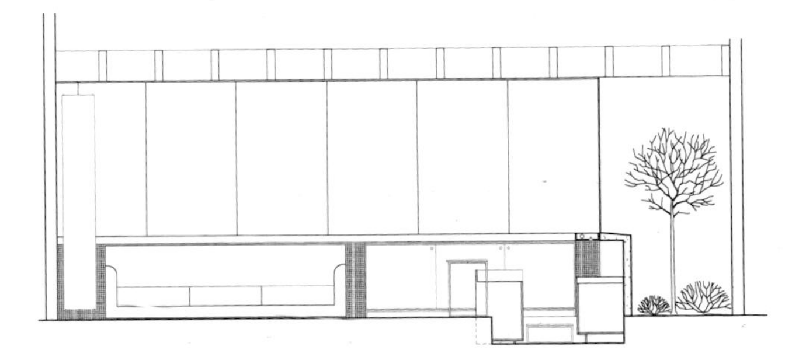

Interior elevation

Meteorit

Propeller Z | Essen

Meteorit is a playful cultural complex that hosts exhibitions and complementary activities. The space is made up of three zones that are differentiated by their location and function: one for exhibitions, another for the bar services and employee quarters, and a third for a store and a cloatroom.

The exhibition area is almost completely submerged in the site. Due to its irregular geometry and peculiar position, its dimensions are ambiguous until the visitor actually enters the area. The 40 feet that separate the hallway from the exhibition hall give an indication of the project's grandeur. A system of ramps, bridges, and stairs connect the different spaces. At the end of the passageway, a mechanical staircase carries the visitor to the entrance, where a hung staircase leads to the café.

The bar is located on a 145 feet platform that progressively rises up from the floor, reaching a height of 95 feet with a three percent incline. The platform is closed by a curved aluminum volume. There is only one open façade, which contains large windows that illuminate the site. The windows are protected by a system of aluminum slats that follow the quartering of the closure. A glass door connects the bar to a wooden terrace, so that it can be extended outdoors when the weather permits. An inclined covering of glass extends from the platform to the floor, making the entrance and the store totally visible from the exterior.

A bowed glass roof spreads from the plataform to the ground and involves entrance and shop areas, both visible from outside

Architects: Propeller Z

Collaborator: André Heller

Photographer: Margherita Spiluttini

Address: Essen, Germany

Opening date: 1998

Surface area: 4,839 sq. feet

Special requisites determined the lighting of the complex at night and inside the premises. On the exterior, the architects tried to create a system that would highlight the qualities of the metals used. Inside, lights and projections mix to emphasize the exposed elements.

When approaching the exhibition space of exhibitions, the visitor first sees an impressive 40 feet empty space. A complicated mosaic of mirrors, with different sizes and orientations, offers distinct perceptions of the lobby. The impact of the lighting also creates numerous visual effects.

Weninger

Propeller Z | Horitschon

To improve the services of this old wine cellar, the space was completely remodeled to include a small gastronomic bar, as well as a store, an office, and a guest bedroom. The building that houses the bodega is a typical farm structure of the region: located between two streets and with an elongated form so that the functions are grouped in a longitudinal manner.

As a result of the building's activity, winemaking, temperature requirements were a determining factor in the project's design. The architects recovered the building's only opening, the southern façade, with glass. To control the entry of light on the ground floor, this surface was shielded with aluminum panels that function as blinds and solar reflectors. Controlled by sensors, the panels can reflect light up to 33 feet, the depth of the interior space. On the upper floor, the façade was covered with a structure made of chipboard wood in order to shade the interior. This structure is used as a balcony on the exterior. To achieve better thermal absorption in the walls, the architects used concrete blocks that also guarantee a constant temperature in the cellar.

A minimal intervention, in a sober language, radically changed the image of this winery

The relationship between the store-bar and the bodega, located in the cellar, is achieved through two openings forged out of wood that divide the two spaces. The rear opening visually relates the areas and permits natural and artificial lighting to unify them. The other opening incorporates a wooden staircase that connects the two floors. Another element that emphasizes the connection between the two spaces is a concrete box that acts as a handrail on the upper floor.

Architects: Propeller Z, Raimund Dickinger

Collaborators: Karl Schemmel (structure); Klaus Pokorny/Equation Lighting Design & Halotech (lighting)

Photographer: Pez Hejduk

Address: Florianigasse 11, 7312 Horitschon, Austria

Opening date: May 1999

Surface area: 806 sq. feet

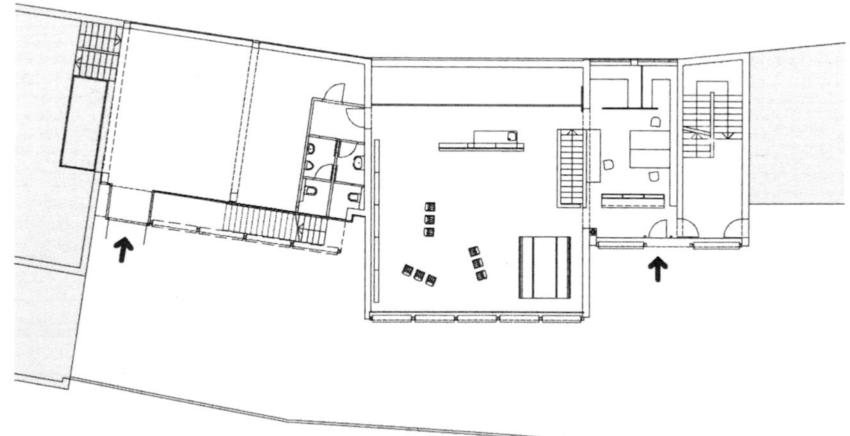

Plan

◀
Thermal conditions and lighting were both important considerations due to the wine cellar in the basement.

◀
Outside and interior materials reflect the noble character of the project. Steel, concrete, glass and wood are combined to create a pure and functional space.

Albion

Wood & Carlos Zapata | Miami

The Albion is a hotel located in the popular zone of South Beach in Miami. The hotel and its bar, of the same name, are situated in the heart of the city's Art Deco district. While the building's exterior conserves its original 30's character, the interior was completely reformed in 1997 to create a new and totally contemporary image. The bar and the hotel were designed by the same architects, who followed certain principles and reinterpreted the distinctive geometric lines from the structure's original era.

The formal language of the interior could be defined as a program of folds, imbalances, and ruptures of the materials. Each architectural element, including the columns, the ceiling, and the walls, breaks apart and forms fissures and transparencies that enrich the space, which has a regular form and reduced dimensions. A continuous floor covers the entire space without any type of division and is a unifying element. On the other hand, glass screens and wooden panels create translucent barriers that define compartments within the space. Fissures in the false ceiling break the column's axis in different directions, forming folds of material that give a feeling of lightness.

This bar features a contrast between different materials and textures, incorporating both classic and contemporary elements

The mixture of textures and colors in the Albion bar creates a sober yet comfortable atmosphere, similar to that of the hotel's ground floor. The cold finishes, like concrete, plaster, and glass, mix with warm elements such as the natural-colored leather upholstery on the chairs and the wood of the panels, the bartop, and the tables. The lamps, an allegory to classic design, are the final decorative touch.

Architect: Wood & Carlos Zapata

Collaborators: Rubell family

Photographer: Pep Escoda

Address: 1650 James Avenue at Lincoln Road, Miami Beach, Florida, USA

Opening date: February 1997

Surface area: 1,290 sq. feet

MATERIAL WORLD

The imbalance of the wooden panels and glass dividers generates deceptive reflections; it also provides visibility of the public areas of the hotel.

Astro Bar

Michael Young | Reykjavik

This project, awarded to the prestigious British designer Michael Young, consisted in reforming one of Reykjavik's legendary discotheques. The club is located in a building that dates to the beginning of the 20th century and its remodeling was subject to strict rules. Young's first challenge was to determine the existing geometry in order to be able to create new environs in an effective manner and without breaking any restriction.

The designer's main objectives were to create an atmosphere conducive to amusement and to breathe enthusiasm and freshness into all the nightclub's zones, including four bars and two dance floors. To accomplish this, Young relied on Icelandic artisan techniques that he admired, such as the manipulation of concrete and steel in the construction of thermal zones. Young's idea was to develop the concept of a picnic zone and a swimming pool. Astro Bar is an interior space that uses outdoor mechanisms in an attempt to evoke the wind and the cold that are so characteristic of the zone.

The Astro Bar balances traditional, indigenous construction systems with pieces of contemporary furniture designed by prestigious firms.

Young carefully selected the furnishings and paid special attention to the finishes of the walls, floor, and ceilings. Capellini and Sawaya & Moroni designed exclusive pieces for the discotheque and Eurolounge created the lights that produce an almost surreal atmosphere.

The upper floor was conceived in a totally distinct manner: as a tranquil, relaxed, and intimate space. In the red lounge, reserved for VIPs, the Thermal Company created a lighting system in the partition walls that reacts to movement. It starts with a pink light that progressively becomes red when there is an increase of physical activity.

Designer: Michael Young

Photographer: Ari Magg

Address: Austurstraeti 22, Reikjavik, Iceland

Opening date: April 2000

Surface area: 2,043 sq. feet

▲
Careful attention was paid to the construction details, including the intersection of distinct elements and the arrangement of the electrical installations.

Lighting plays such an important role in nightclubs that Michael Young designed special lamps to create an extensive variety of perceptions.

While the ground floor is the setting for the typical bustle of a dance club, the second floor was designed as a space for relaxation a place to converse and to escape the noise and frenetic movement below.

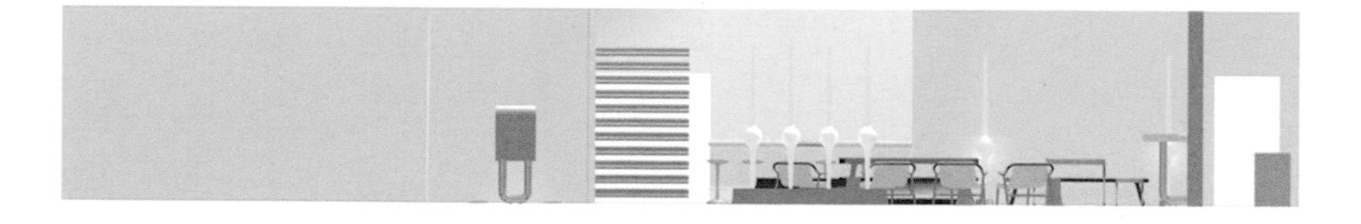

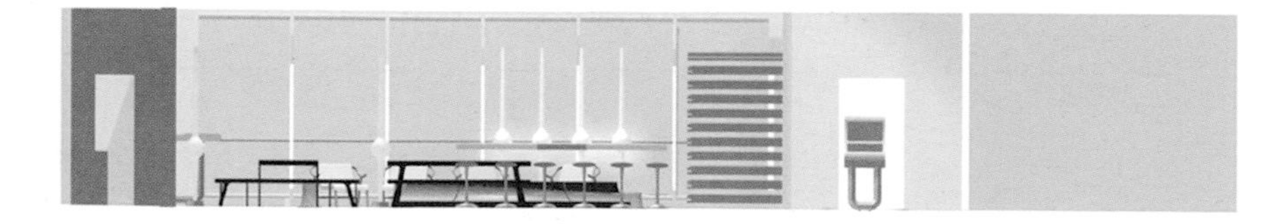

Interior elevations

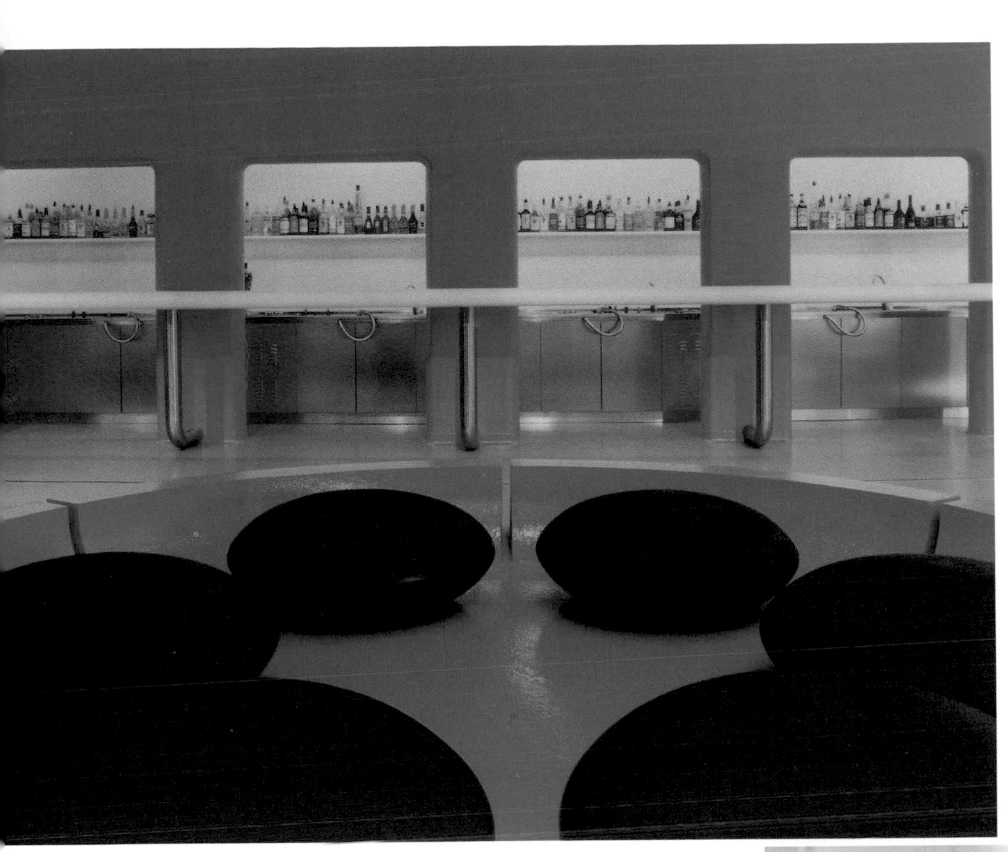

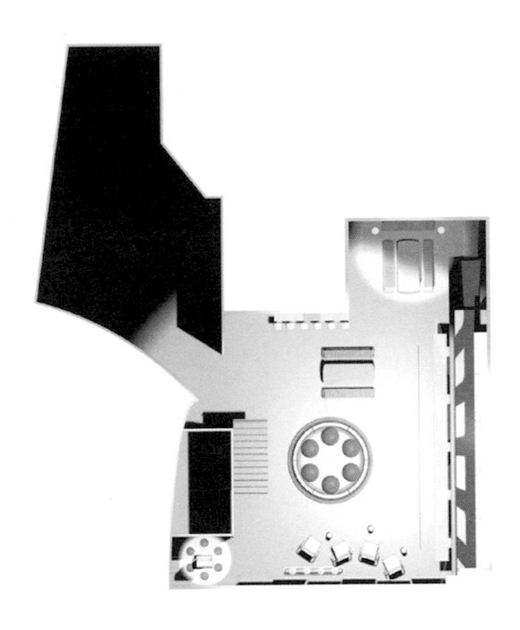

Lower floor

The rounded forms of the architectural elements, the furnishings, and the accessories create a homogeneous atmosphere diversified by the color of the finishes.

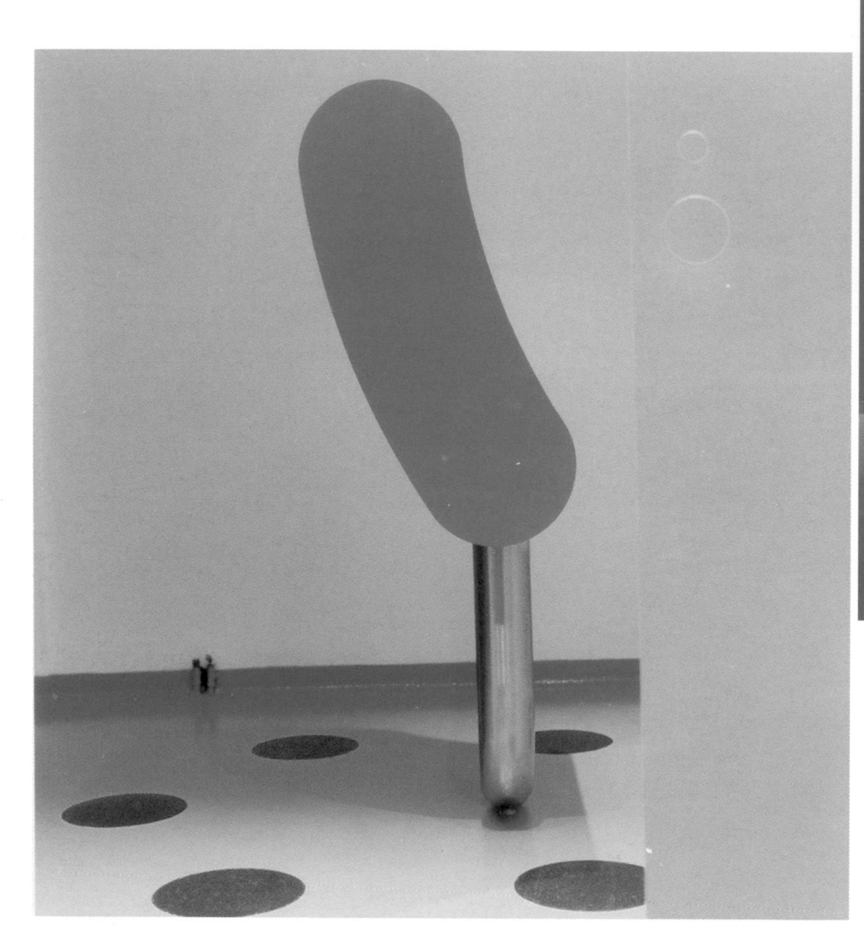

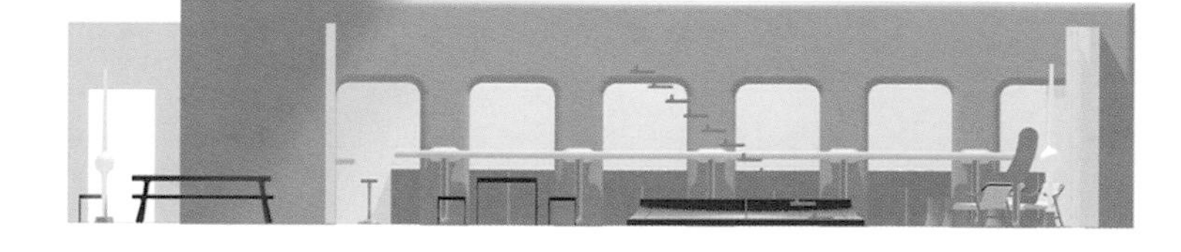

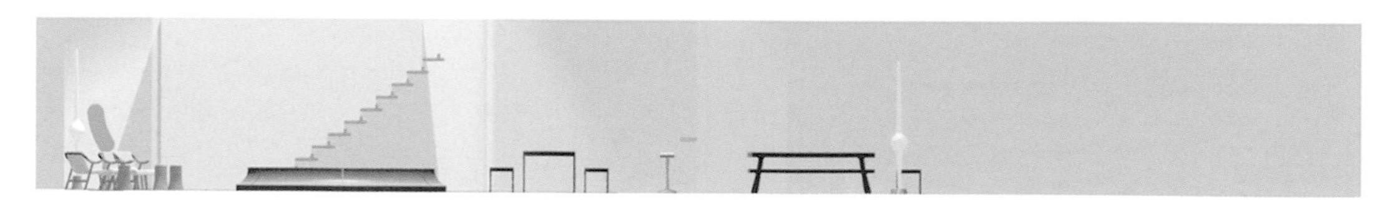

Interior sections

Dietrich

Dani Freixes | **Berlin**

The Dietrich is the hotel bar of the Grand Hyatt in Berlin. Located in front of the plaza Marlene Dietrich, for which it is named, the bar is situated in one of Berlin's most attractive and strategic enclaves, the Potsdamer Platz.

The work of architect Dani Freixes and the rest of the team was influenced by several key factors: the space's dimensions (almost 1,440 sq. feet), the generous height of the ceilings (13 feet), its corner location, and the irregularity of its forms.

The bar was conceived as the meeting point between the hotel and the street, and both spaces have double access to the Dietrich. The architects opted to design a simple plan that meets the basic needs of this type of setting, which is meant to function first as a *noodles* bar, then as a Russian food restaurant, and finally as a beer hall with fast food.

Over the bar, the architects hung an inclined mirror that gives a full view of the kitchen. Located just behind the bar, the kitchen features stainless steel, a material that is more modern and easier to clean than wood. Tables are located on the other side of the bar. In this zone, the architects repeated the combination of steel and wood, materials that manage to create a warm and elegant atmosphere, strengthened by a careful lighting strategy that mixes distinct sources of light.

The false wooden ceilings suspended from the roof emphasize the relationship between interior and exterior

Architect: Dani Freixes, Varis Arquitectes

Collaborators: Vicente Miranda, Vicenç Bou, and Lali González

Photographer: Mihail Moldoveanu

Address: Grand Hyatt Hotel, Potsdamer Platz, Berlin, Germany

Opening date: December 1998

Surface area: 1,440 sq. feet

DIETRICH'S
BISTRO

The two accesses to the bar were resolved in the same way: a cross section of woodwork with aluminum and glass panels. In the case of the entrance that leads to the street, the door can be covered with theatrical red curtains that show off the ceiling's generous height while insulating the interior during the coldest months of the year.

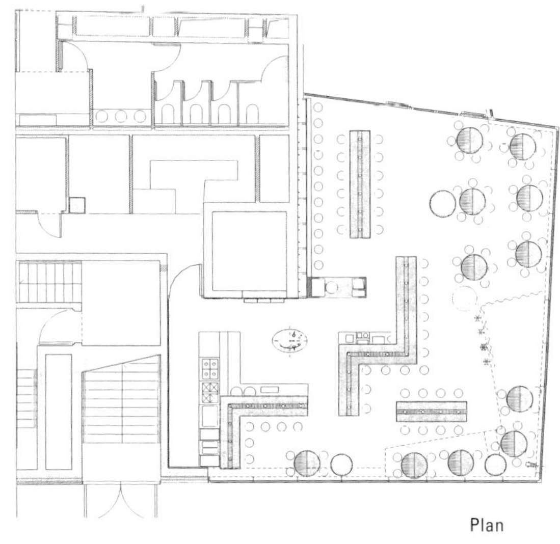

Plan

Siam

Guillermo Arias | Bogotá

This bar is located in an ancient colonial house in the old quarter of La Candelaria in Bogotá. The project included all the spaces in the house, as well as the long garden in the back. The remodeling sought to respect the original structure as much as possible.

The entrance is a narrow corridor that leads to a patio. This patio is the organizing point for the rest of the spaces, since the bathrooms, the cloatroom, the main room, and a VIP room are situated around it. In the main room, the architect elevated the ceiling to obtain more height and created an access to the garden in the back, where there is another bar. He also specially designed the furnishings and the lamps in the VIP room. The main room and the VIP room conserve the original finish of the walls and the original structure of the ceiling, made of wood, cane, and mud tiles.

The new and the old combine in an atmosphere of suggestive lights and shadows

The rooms toward the street are used for the bathrooms and have a great formal expressiveness. The walls that define the areas are painted in strong colors, do not reach the ceiling, and are separated from the existing walls. Areas for handwashing are made of smooth concrete and are integrated with the social areas of the bar. One of them is connected to the entrance hallway by way of an opening in the wall, allowing the visitor to see the hands behind it. The other one is linked to the central patio with a single wall.

The garden's irregular form was remedied through the use of a continuous floor and large porticos that link it to the interior. The residual space was used for vegetation that can be enjoyed from a balcony on the upper part.

Architect: Guillermo Arias

Collaborator: Christophe Chavarriat

Photographer: Claudia Uribe/AXXIS

Address: Calle 9 Cra 2 Este, Bogotá, Colombia

Opening date: September 2000

Surface area: 2,688 sq. feet

The lighting was carefully studied to emphasize the project's characteristics. In the service zones, light fixtures frame the difference between new and old elements. In the main room and in the VIP room, they generate a homogeneous and warm atmosphere.

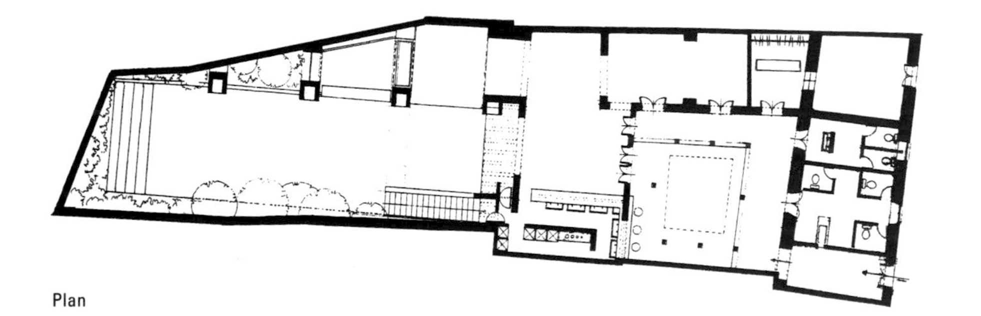

Plan

The contrast between the original structure and incorporated elements stands out by the difference in colour. The washbasins and the other pieces of the bathroom were designed and constructed during the project.

Grade

Hugo Vanneste | **Ghent**

This bar, located in the center of Ghent, was part of an expansion of the restaurant next door, to which it has direct access. The site is situated in front of the city's l argest park in the middle of the museum district. The first step was to paint the three levels of the façade of the two houses in black to make a strong statement on the exterior. This strategy respects the buildings' original characters yet makes them stand out among the other buildings in the area.

The Grade bar was designed in the same spirit as the restaurant — a combination of contemporary style and nostalgia. The bar complements the restaurant by giving it a light touch of lounge culture. The architect made the most of the space's narrow proportions by conceiving and designing the bar as a free flow of ambiences and impressions. The barriers between public and private areas fade so that clients can enjoy every action that takes place. For example, the activity of the waiters and the opening and closing of the refrigerator doors are an important part of the public's experience.

Grade presents a mix of visual images and tactile experiences with the aim of stimulating the public's senses

During the expansion, the old entrance to the restaurant was removed and an access was created through the bar. Made of two rooms in an old house, the bar is a rectangular space and a lounge with a terrace at the end of the hallway.

The materials and final details emphasize and enrich the contrast between the original structure and the new remodeling. Linear pieces that cross the space dominate the main room, which features stainless steel refrigerators, glass shelves, a lateral wall, and a wood bar. Natural stone from India is arranged in an irregular form on the floor.

Architect: Hugo Vanneste

Collaborators: Steven Wittouck

Photographer: Bart Van Leuven

Address: Charles de Kerchovelaan 79/81, Ghent, Belgium

Opening date: September 2001

Surface area: 2,182 sq. feet

The composition of the black color of the façade is 40 percent red, resulting in a warm tone that frames the surroundings. The back façade is defined by a continual piece of glass that links the main room to the terrace. The relationship between these two areas is further emphasized by the continuous natural stone floor.

The two original rooms conserve the house's character, which contrasts with the furnishings and the modern decor. A large baseboard made of a wooden panel acts as the backrest of a continuous bench and is the nexus between the two styles.

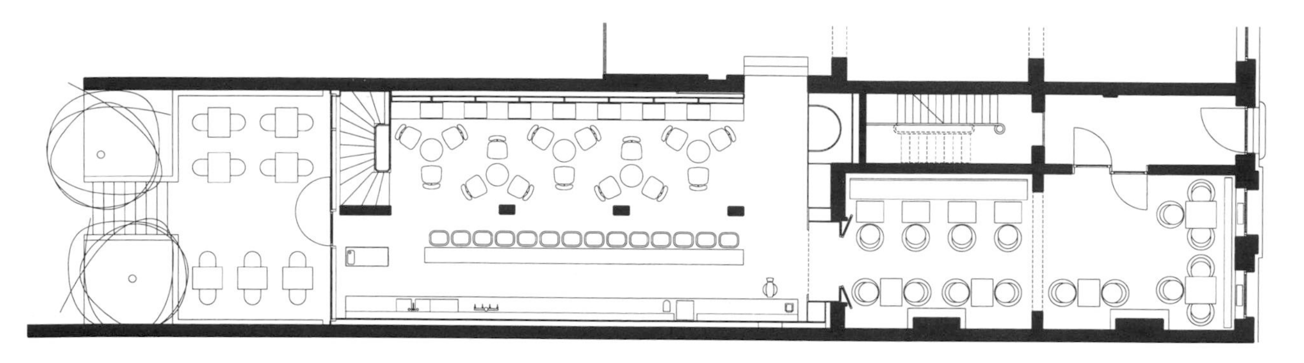

Plan

Charles and Ray Eames designed the chairs in the main room, while the Hi-Pad benches at the bar are a creation of Jasper Morrison. The benches change position according to the movement of the public.

Bars and Restaurants

BED

Oliver & Pascale Hoyos | Miami

The principle behind the design of BED was to create a comfortable and intimate atmosphere that reflects a hedonistic culture. BED offers the visitor luxurious and pleasurable surroundings, as well as a studied collection of music, entertainment, and first-class gourmet cuisine. The name sums it up: Beverage, Entertainment, and Dining, all of which are featured in this innovative interior space.

There are no tables or chairs in BED Instead, the setting accommodates 150 people in beds on elevated platforms. The size of the beds can be adjusted according to the size of the group and can fit for private groups of up to 90 people. White translucent curtains separate the gatherings, giving each group privacy. The beds are mainly situated on the sides of the rectangular space that includes the bar. Enormous lengthwise sofas cover the area, while three independent beds are placed in the center.

BED is a delicate setting with subtle romantic references for a repertoire of music, food, and entertainment

The decorative details, as well as the technical elements implemented in the project's design, complement the beds' strong presence, creating a special ambience. Numerous projectors show images throughout the salon and a central screen displays a constantly changing exhibition of colors and pictures. A selection of famous DJs work with the latest sound technology, which is also used for the presentation of live music.

Details, such as handmade rugs that cover the platforms and natural fiber cloths that cover the beds, enrich the space. The pillows were designed by Oliver and Pascale Hoyos.

Designers: Oliver & Pascale Hoyos

Photographer: Pep Escoda

Address: 929 Washington Av., Miami Beach, Florida, USA

Opening date: November 1999

Surface area: 2,365 sq. feet

The furnishings are Middle Eastern Style and create the atmosphere of an oasis in the middle of the desert. Advanced lighting and sound technology help make this a place of multiple sensations.

Aureole

Adam Tihany | **Las Vegas**

Anyone who enters the door of Aureole is captivated by this spectacular stainless steel and glass building that reaches almost 510 feet and is four stories high and four stories wide. Yet it's the way the restaurant's wine is organized that leaves clients spellbound.

Inspired by a scene in the film "Mission Impossible" in which Tom Cruise, held by harnesses, descends from the ceiling, the architect Adam Tihany designed an original twist on the wine cellar in which the waiters bring down bottles of wines using an ingeniuous mechanism of mechanical pulleys. Tihany's idea is as functional as it is theatrical, and Aureole has quickly become one of the most popular eating establishments in Las Vegas.

Built as a restaurant for the new Millennium, Aureole is the jewel in the crown of Mandalay Bay, one of the most luxurious complexes in town. The spacious, multi-function restaurant is divided into different areas dedicated to different activities. Five separate spaces are carved out of the more than 9,100 square feet: the bar, called "The Lounge," two central dining rooms - known as the "Main Room" and "Aureole Swan Court" — and three private dining rooms, named "Terrace Room," "Board Room," and "Center Room." Each of these spaces has its own personality. Tihany has an unmistakable style and the attention he pays to architectural and decorative details gives the practical yet beautiful interiors a feeling of luxury, sophistication, and modernity.

The bar surrounds a high steel and glass structure that towers over the whole space

Architect: Adam Tihany

Photographer: Mark Ballogg

Adress: Mandalay Bay, Las Vegas, Estados Unidos

Opening date: marzo de 1999

Surface area: 9,182 sq. feet

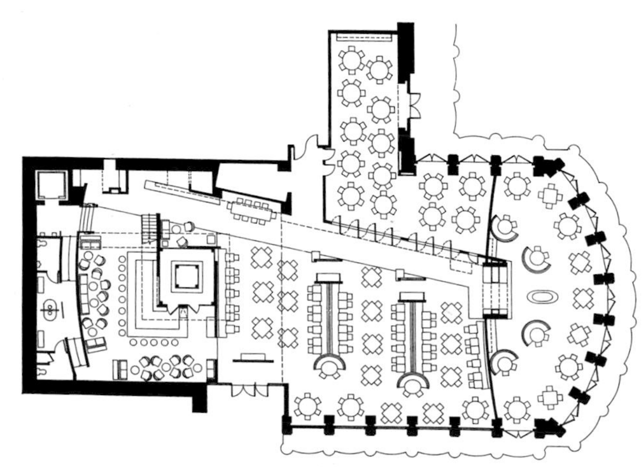

Ground floor

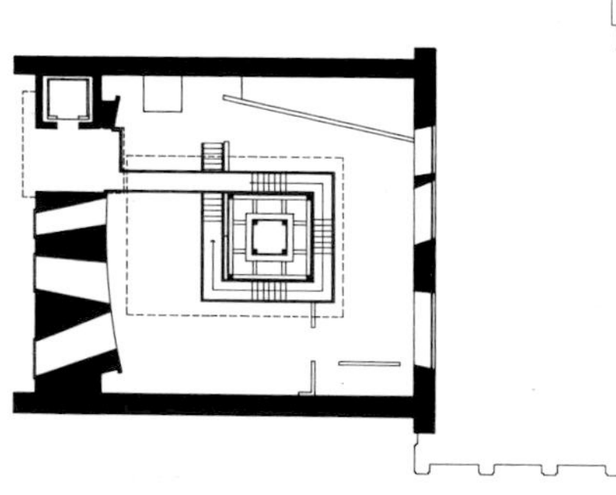

Second floor

Three elements combine to create Aureole's distinguished, elegant atmosphere: a careful selection of materials, chromatic combinations strengthened by appropriate lighting, and an interesting mix of decorative details.

Nicole Fahri

Gabellini Associates | New York

This restaurant-bar is part of a large-format boutique that occupies three floors of an emblematic building dating to 1901 in the upper part of Manhattan. Situated between Madison and Fifth Avenue, the building is only a few steps away from Central Park. The store's 21,500 sq. feet are divided into departments for men, women, home décor, and the restaurant-bar, which takes up a third of the total area on the lower floor.

The exterior of this building, until recently the site of the famous nightclub Copa Cabana, was completelyrestored. Pieces of limestone and granite that existed in the original drawings were reproduced. The new windows and the store's entrance were designed in bronze and white opaque glass to complement the character of the original architecture.

Visitors access the building by way of a suspended bridge made of walnut and glass that eliminated the need for plasterwork on the interior of the façade. From the bridge, one can perceive the entire space. The staircase, made of the same materials as the bridge, is visible from the left and leads down to the lower level where the bar and restaurant are located. To the right, in the upper part of the double-height space, what stands out is a luminous bar top made out of Estremosz, a Portuguese marble selected for its translucency and subtle veins.

The diverse functions of Nicole Farhi, as a clothing store and as a bar-restaurant, led to the idea of a setting with diverse spatial relations

In addition to the spatial configurations that link the store and the restaurant, other elements and materials connect the two areas. The oval columns are repeated and emphasized as individual elements in the two atmospheres. The use of opaque glass, walnut wood, and natural stone also strengthens the connection.

Architects: Gabellini Associates

Photographer: Paul Warchol

Address: 14 East 60th Street, New York, USA

Opening date: June 1999

Surface area: 1,397 sq. feet

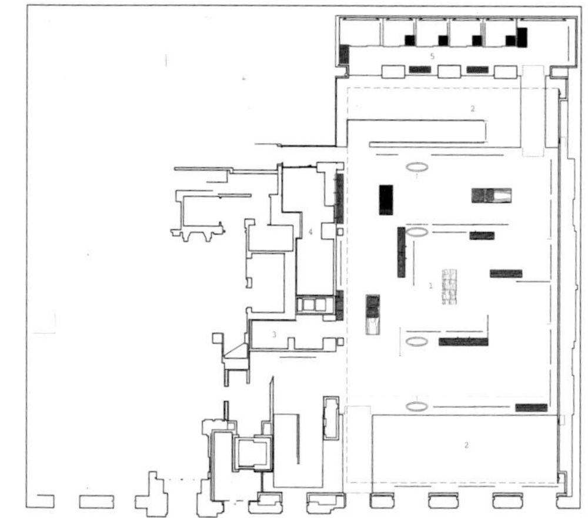

Main access

Lower level

The clothing store is located on the ground floor, while the restaurant occupies the lower level. The relationship between the two spaces is evident from the moment the visitor crosses the bridge, from which it is possible to see the entire locale.

The palette of white and gray tones highlights the wood and stone work while creating a sober and tranquil atmosphere.

Pearl

Stephan Dupoux | Miami

Full of color, this restaurant-bar is located in the heart of South Beach in Miami. More than a restaurant, it is an aesthetic reference for this effervescent zone of urban activity, fashion, and design. Pearl is the mixture of a bar and a restaurant that specializes in champagne. The designer achieved the sophisticated ambience with few materials, sensual forms, and a careful lighting strategy that accentuates the space's dominating color palette. The project's objective was to create an atmosphere for relaxation while giving the visitor the sensation of "seeing and being seen."

The color that characterizes the space inspired its name. A gray pearl tone coats the tables and the chairs and most of the background walls. Against this backdrop, a recurring decorative theme is the use of tall curtains suspended from the ceiling that divide the space and create textures and transparencies. The resulting atmosphere, with few elements, comes from the combination of amber lighting and reflecting and translucent materials that produce interesting textures.

The sophistication of this ambience is achieved through homogeneous, daring lighting that dominates the space

The furnishings in the dining room were inspired by American cafés of the 40´s and 50's, in a salute to the golden age of Miami's Art Deco district. The bar stools, yet another distinctive element of Pearl, recall the Futurism of the 60's and 70's. Low sofas and soft armchairs also create a variety of situations within the same warm atmosphere.

Designer: Stephan Dupoux

Photographer: Pep Escoda

Address: 1 Ocean Drive, Miami, Florida, USA

Opening date: 2000

Surface area: 1,505 sq. feet

▲
The repetition of elements creates textures that are also used for decoration. The curtains and the lamps that are repeated in the niches of a wall also serve as lighting sources and important decorative details.

▲
The diverse furnishings create various situations within the space, taking center stage in some zones and establishing the most private and intimate setting in others.

EXIT

Bar og Restaurant

Kristin Jarmund | **Oslo**

This space, situated in a neoclassic building from the 20´s, was originally designed as the lobby of a hotel and was later converted into a food store. In 1997, architects completely reformed the space and transformed it into the Bar og Restaurant.

The challenge was to create a place that combines the functions of a bar and restaurant and that balances a continental atmosphere with modern trends. The architects sought the sensation of a timeless space with an intimate ambience and a contemporary language. The architectural team replaced the openings of the façade on the lower floor of the building with large glass windows that border the space towards the street. The windows can be elevated with motors so that the restaurant can become completely integrated with the exterior and form part of the urban activity.

The original construction plays an important role in the design. The large, existing columns and the space's vertical tendency contrast with the horizontal loft

To make the most of the interior's spatial possibilities, the dining room ceiling is two stories high while the back part is defined by a bar and loft in a curved form. The two levels at the back create a more intimate atmosphere. From the loft, it's possible to see the activity of the restaurant and kitchen. An ideal place for more private receptions, the loft offers a view of the entire locale.

The materials and colors that the architects used are meant to create a balance between an open, fluid space and a warm atmosphere. The floor is of natural slate and the walls combine mahogany panels with plaster finishes painted white, gray, and coral red. The complementary details are stainless steel and glass. Philippe Stark designed the furnishings.

Architect: Kristin Jarmund, Einar Sandbaek

Collaborators: Ola Helle, Lise Meiner, and Steffen Emhjellen

Photographer: Jiri Havran

Address: Kirkeveien 64, 0364 Oslo, Norway

Opening date: September 1998

Surface area: 5,107 sq. feet

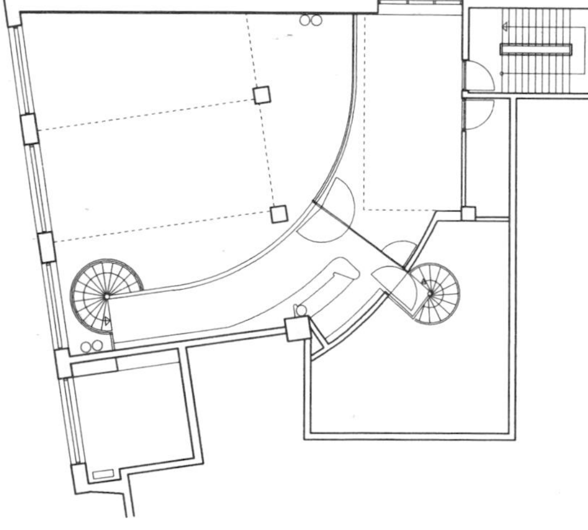

Ground floor

Mezzanine

The clientele and the service change from midday to night, when the natural light is replaced by artificial. Sources of visible light, including lamps and indirect fixtures, combine and adjust to create different atmospheres that set the mood according to the moment.

The loft structure is suspended from the upper floor with 1 inch steel cables. This solution avoids columns on the lower floor and gives the space a certain expressiveness.

▲
El aire fresco se reparte por el local gracias a una cámara instalada en el falso techo. Con este sistema se logró ganar la máxima altura dentro del restaurante y evitar que los conductos de ventilación quedaran a la vista.

Fresh air flows throughout the restaurant by way of a chamber hung in the false ceiling. With this system, the restaurant reached its maximum height and the ventilation ducts are concealed.

L'Industrial

BSB Associats | Girona

The requirements of the industrial area in which this restaurant-bar is located were the starting point for this project. The surrounding environment includes a series of structures without any particular order. The architects incorporated some elements of composition from this setting and aimed to create a refuge from the chaos. The interior design seeks to balance the industrial requirements with more playful qualities. L´Industrial is a pleasant, spacious restaurant that invites workers in the area to take a break. The design also establishes a harmonious relationship with the surroundings.

The physical space defined the layout of the different elements that make up the interior space. The setting is rectangular-shaped and has ample proportions, highceilings, and an enormous window that looks to the exterior on one side. On the other side is a longitudinal bar and an inclined false ceiling made of colored wood that emphasizes the relationship with the exterior.

The qualities of each material stand out thanks to the attention paid to details and the absence of ornamentation

The architects sought, with technical engineering and clever solutions, to transmit a sensation of well-being through the use of elements with an industrial origin. A gold-colored and wavy metal sheet rounds off the back part of the restaurant and gives the appearance of a large theater curtain.

The restaurant's industrial character is emphasized by the exposed air conditioning ducts, the suspended lamps, and the fluorescent tubes of the false ceiling in the bar. The wooden cabinets, tables, and chairs generate a warm and cozy atmosphere.

Architect: Antoni Bramon, Lluís Sitjà, Jesús Bassols, and Maite Prats, interior designer

Collaborator: Maite Prats (interiorismo)

Photographer: Eugeni Pons

Address: Calle G, Polígono Industrial Pont-Xetmar, Girona, Spain

Opening date: March 2000

Surface area: 2,118 sq. feet

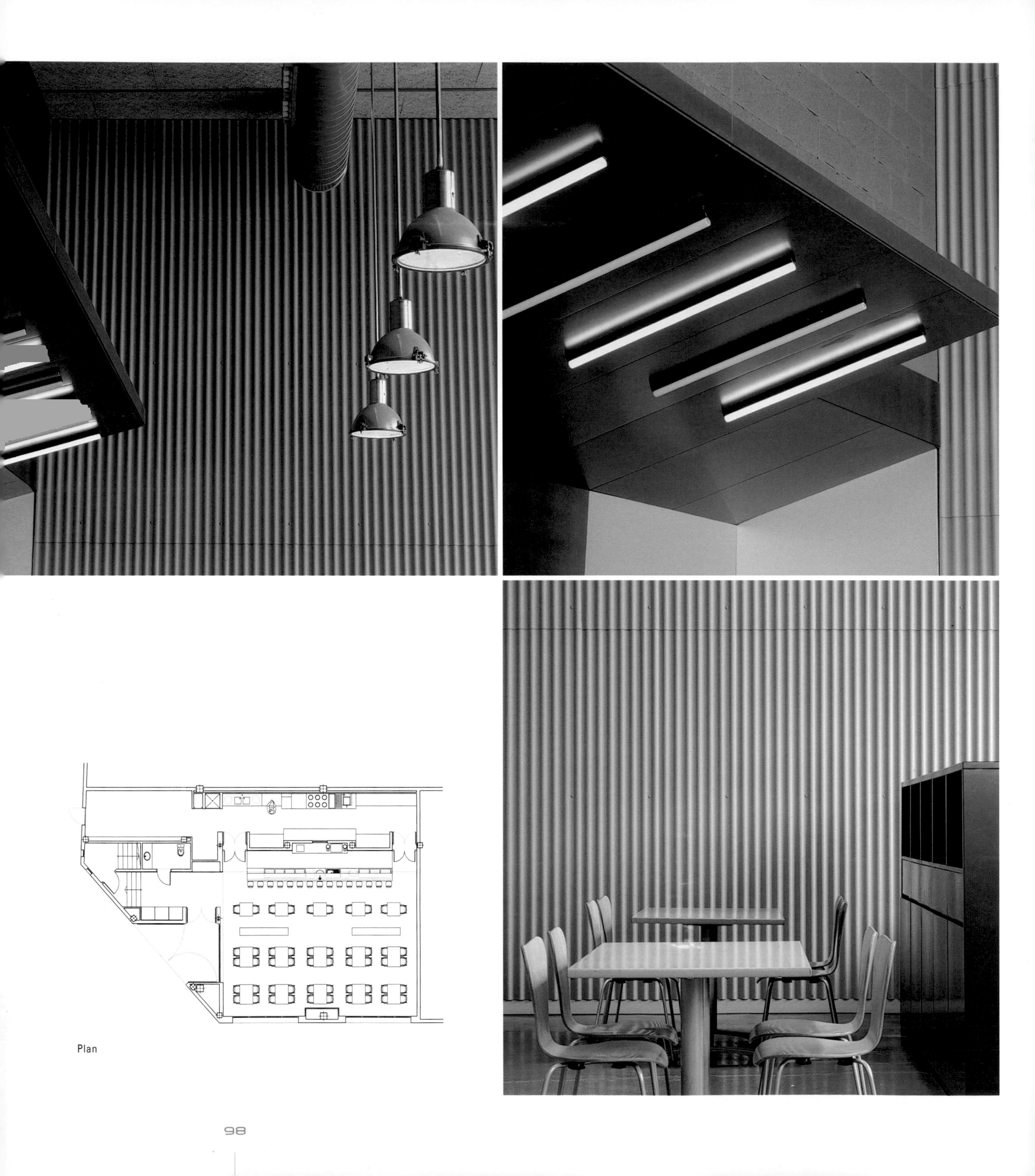

Plan

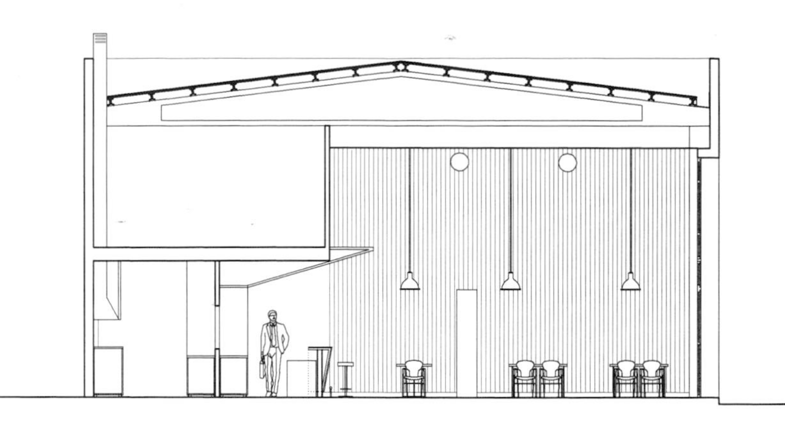

Transversal section

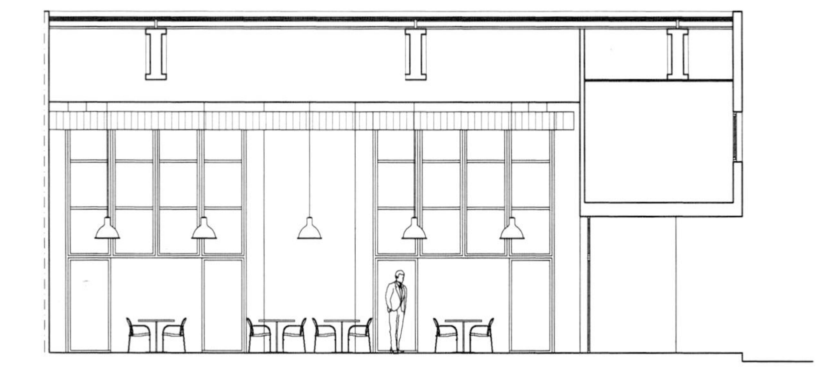

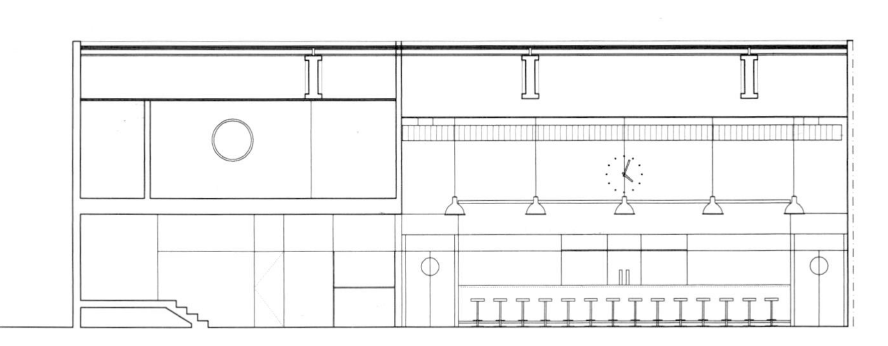

Longitudinal section

▲ The architects managed to create a tranquil, relaxed space with few elements, noble materials, and a palette of earth and gray tones. The linen stations, which also have shelves for wine, divide the space and frame the passageways.

Costa Smeralda

Peter Marino | **Costa Smeralda**

This club, originally constructed in 1977, is a 62,000 sq. feet complex comprised of various lounges and suites. As a whole, the building reflects a strong nautical character, and, thanks to its privileged location, enjoys a spectacular view of Porto Cervo. The foundations of architect Peter Marino's designs were to value the original personality of the space while using a fresh and elegant language.

The club contains nine private suites, eight lounges, a café-bar, a restaurant, a public terrace, and a walkway that partially surrounds the complex. Cherry wood is used for all the architectural elements of the interior, including the floor, the columns, and the ceiling. Cherry is also used as the structural material for the most key furnishings, such as the bar and the semicircular sofas. Marino avoided the use of additional elements that might interrupt spatial continuity with the terrace and block visibility of the landscape.

The interior preserves the nautical character of the original structure and makes the most of the building's spectacular surroundings

The decorative details complement the interior, which has the feel of a ship. Cotton fabrics in different patterns and in blue and white were selected to upholster the chairs and sofas. The folding curtains give the space warmth and act as screens that set the mood by reflecting the light generated by the lamps hidden behind them. In the bar area, three large lamps hang from the ceiling above the semicircular sofas. Other lamps rest on auxiliary tables and floor lamps stand in front of the columns.

Architect: Peter Marino

Collaborators: Enzo Satta; Intertecno (engineer); Luciano Biggio (structure)

Photographer: Andrea Brizzi

Adress: Marina de Porto Cervo, Costa Smeralda, Sardinia, Italy

Opening date: June 2001

Surface area: 62,365 sq. feet

Bar Shu

Fabio Novembre | **Milan**

The Italian architect Fabio Novembre designed this project, which is distinguished by its theatrical and eclectic spirit. The interiors of the bar-restaurant Shu are both poetic and imaginative. The original mixture of trends, ranging from the most avant-garde designs to more sober proposals inspired by the Orient, stirs the imagination and delights the senses of all who visit this fashionable setting in Milan.

The project consists of a multi-functional space in which the 3,500 sq. feet are distributed in a way that makes it possible to carry out various activities without interference. The architect treated the bar area as if it were a restless spatial nave. Metallic materials with visual lightness dominate, and the space is organized around an intriguing and conspicuous bar with generous dimensions that capture the client's attention. Transparent chairs, tables with a steel base and glass top, green neon lights, and a resin floor that imitates green grass transport the visitor to a world in which imagination plays the starring role.

Egyptian mythology and the most avant-garde trends inspire this restaurant in Milan, which merges reality and fiction

Curtains made of rough black velvet are tied to the walls and separate the bar from the restaurant. In the dining area, the bar's futuristic atmosphere is replaced by a Baroque and theatrical ambience. The gigantic gold arms and legs of the Egyptian god SHU rise up from the black floor. SHU, for whom the establishment is named, appears to hold up the sky, which in this case is the restaurant's ceiling.

Architect: Fabio Novembre

Collaborators: Marco Braga, Lorenzo De Nicola

Photographer: Alberto Ferrero

Address: Molino delle Armi Streey, Milan, Italy

Opening date: September 1999

Surface area: 3,548 sq. feet

▲

The bar's light materials, textures, and chromatic neutrality give the space a futuristic and ethereal air that contrasts with the atmosphere in the restaurant, where the materials, colors, and textures have more visual weight. This mixture of styles gives SHU an eclectic flair and great expressive strength.

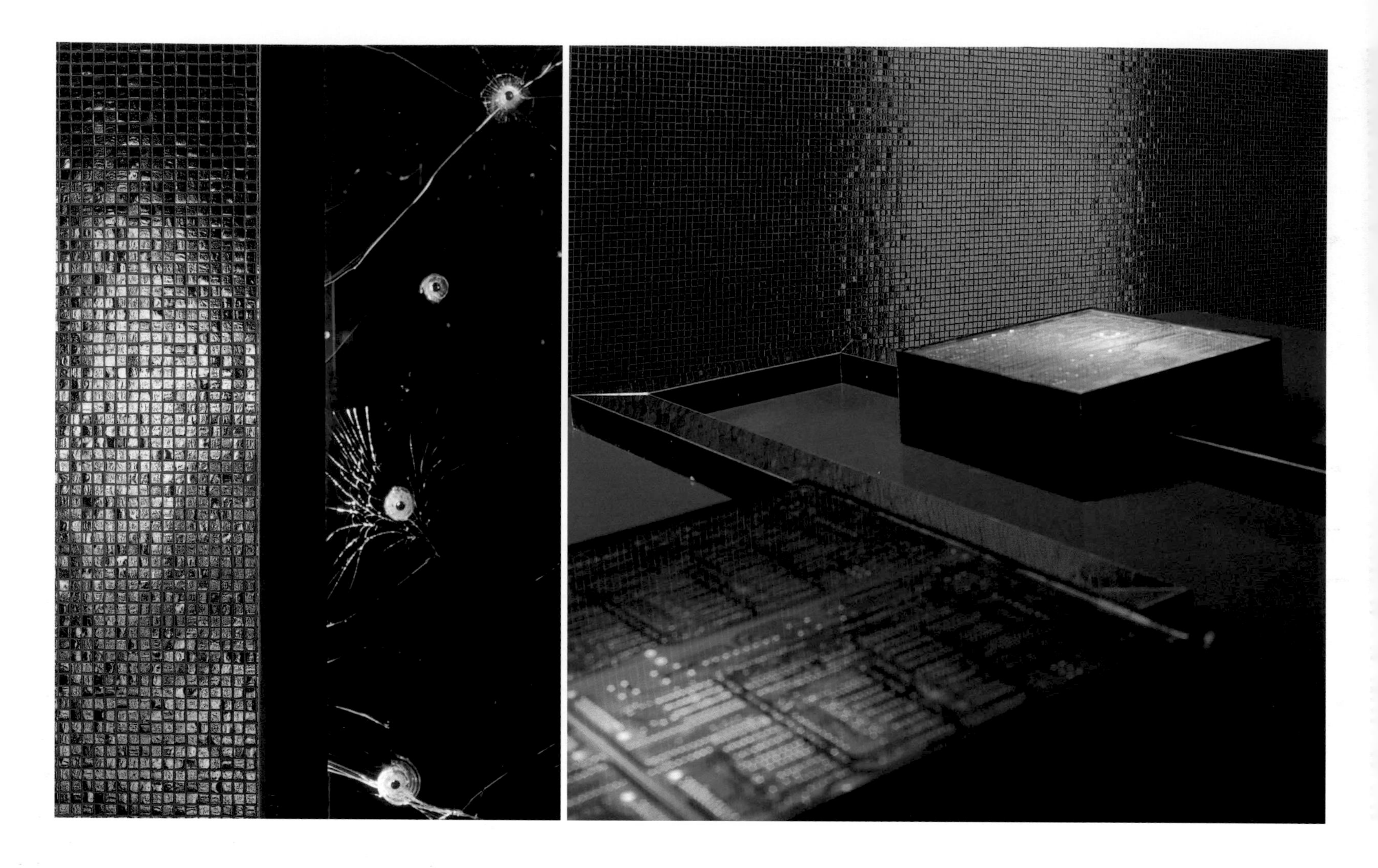

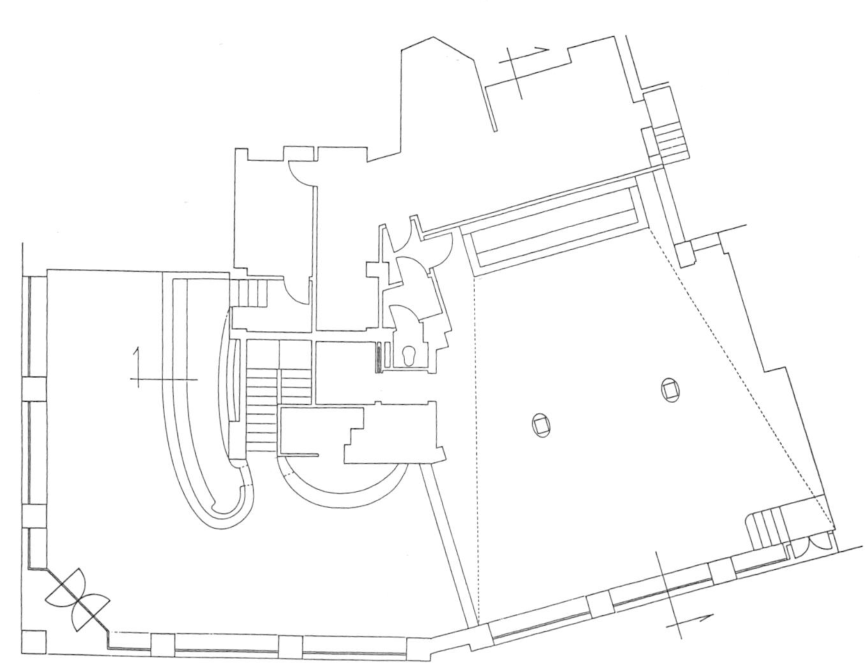

Plan (bar configuration)

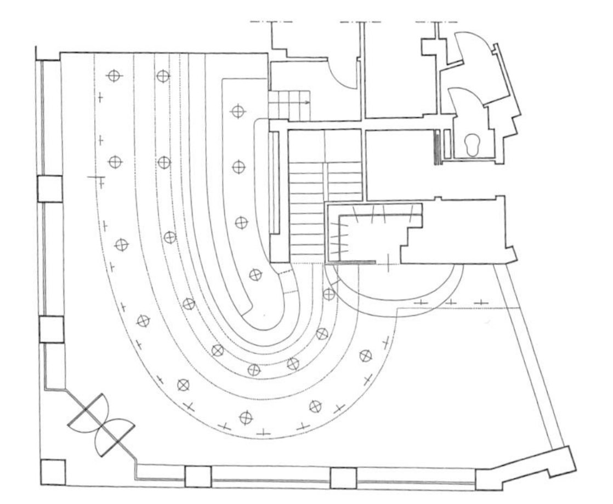

Detail of the bar

Mirrored walls strategically placed around the restaurant manage to create multiple, attractive optical effects. The restaurant's restless atmosphere is further strengthened by the lighting and by the extraordinary decorative solution used on the ceiling.

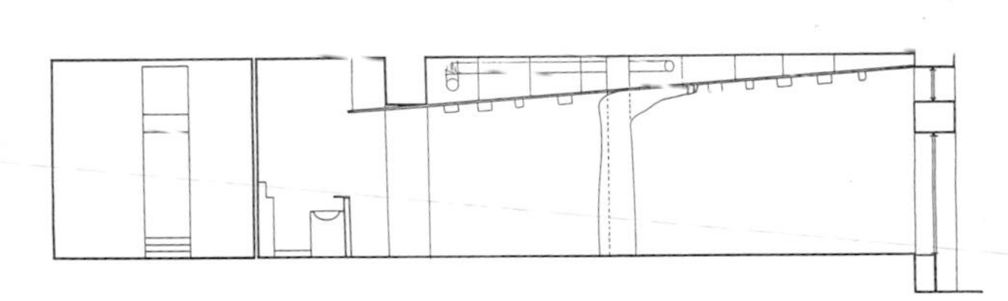

Section

Restaurants

Georges

Jakob & McFarlane | **Paris**

The comprehensive remodeling of the Georges Pompidou Center in Paris included the addition of a new restaurant on the sixth floor. The project had to meet all the requirements of this type of program, while establishing an open relationship with the exterior. The challenge was to respond to these conditions in an architectural context as particular as that of the Pompidou center of art and contemporary culture.

As a starting point, the architect created a type of architecture that, in some ways, emerged from the existing structure and that proposed the most minimal intervention possible. The design team selected the floor as the unifying and base element of the interior design. Viewed as a new work surface, the floor was distorted to the point that a series of volumes appeared underneath it, creating a new landscape of interior and exterior worlds, of hiding places and camouflaged textures. The floor was made out of aluminum to reinforce the idea of a backdrop. Aluminum's shiny finish absorbs and reflects light, which appears and disappears according to the conditions of the space. The floor became a kind of mask, with a strong personality but a discreet presence.

Modulated from the same structure as the building, organic forms create a suggestive interior landscape

The different spaces that make up the restaurant — the kitchen, bar, cloatroom, and private meeting room — are slid underneath the aluminum surface. The spaces are placed in a way to give the perception of movement detained in time, creating an architecture that speaks to the project´s dynamic qualities. As in the rest of the museum, the electrical, hydraulic, and computer installations lead to bubble-shaped compartments wich reinforces the idea of change and flexible, spontaneous systems.

Architects: Jakob & McFarlane

Photographers: Nicolas Borel, Archipress

Address: Place Georges Pompidou, Paris, France

Opening date: February 2000

Surface area: 3,010 sq. feet

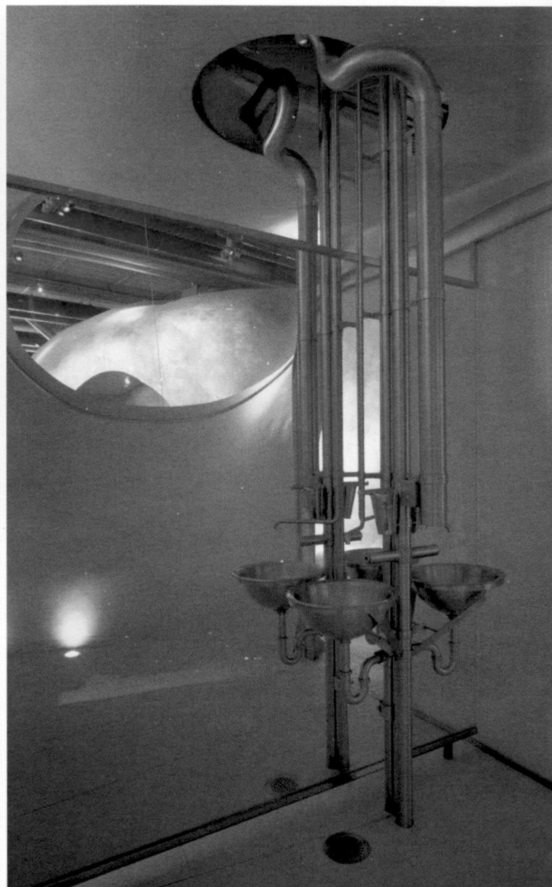

▲

The ambiguity of aluminum, as a texture that appears and disappears according to the intensity of light, contrasts with the distinct character of the compartments, which are distinguished by the predominant color inside them.

The furniture was specially designed for the restaurant in an austere language that avoids references to particular styles or fashions. Its lines, the same height of the terrace, emphasize the relationship between the interior and the exterior.

Tsunami

Morphosis | **Las Vegas**

Las Vegas is a city with a distinct identity. When creating Tsunami, Morphosis, one of the most prestigious architectural studios of today, kept Las Vegas's identity in mind. They also played with the city's image and reinterpreted its special characteristics. The idea was to participate in Las Vegas's game, but to play by different rules.

The objective of the interior design of Tsunami, which specializes in Asian cuisine, was to create a space that spotlights the decor and the exquisite menu of specialties. Morphosis´s idea was to find an intriguing balance between the immateriality of the two-dimensional image and the three-dimensional space. The ultimate goal was to reinterpret the proposals that usually define this style of restaurant. The result is a personal space in which each area is perfectly defined by its decorative solution.

By recycling and repeating an historic style, the architects sought to create an authentic and totally innovative space in which the past and the present flow in a dynamic way

Tsunami was conceived as a space defined by the manipulation of a two-dimensional surface area. In the space designated as the restaurant, a series of volumes and steel panels are pegged to each other and covered with fixed projected images. This innovative solution creates a strong sensation of visual dynamism and spatial fluidity. The murals that cover the surfaces are narrative elements that make the visitor feel like he or she is inside a work of three-dimensional art.

Tsunami is full of personality. Its eclectic atmosphere resulted from a provocative mix of minimalism and frequent allusions to the Asiatic culture and oriental traditions.

Architect: Morphosis

Photographer: Farshid Assassi

Address: 3377 Boulevard South, Las Vegas, Nevada, USA

Opening date: 2000

Surface area: 6,688 sq. feet

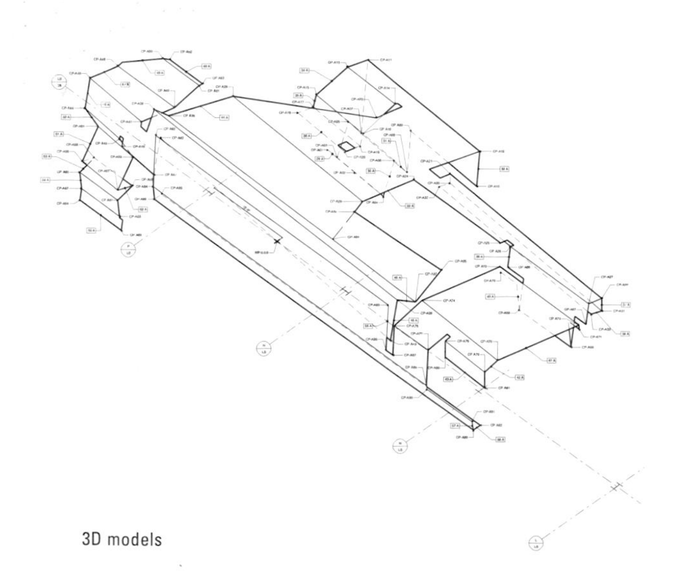

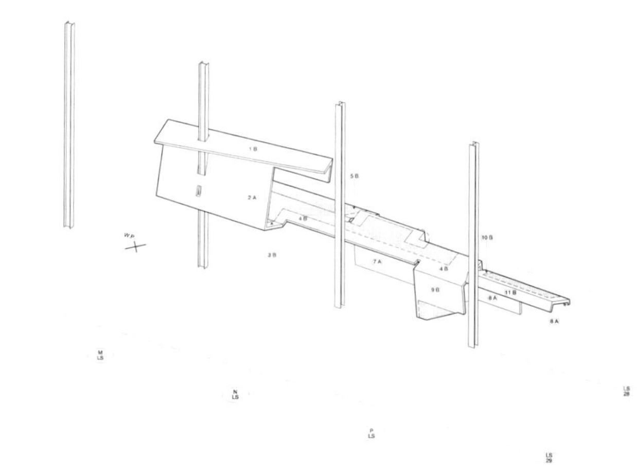

3D models

The result of this intervention achieves a space which can be read in two ways: on one hand, it generates a physical reading due to the architectural solutions it employs, and on the other, alludes to a more figurative and abstract interpretation.

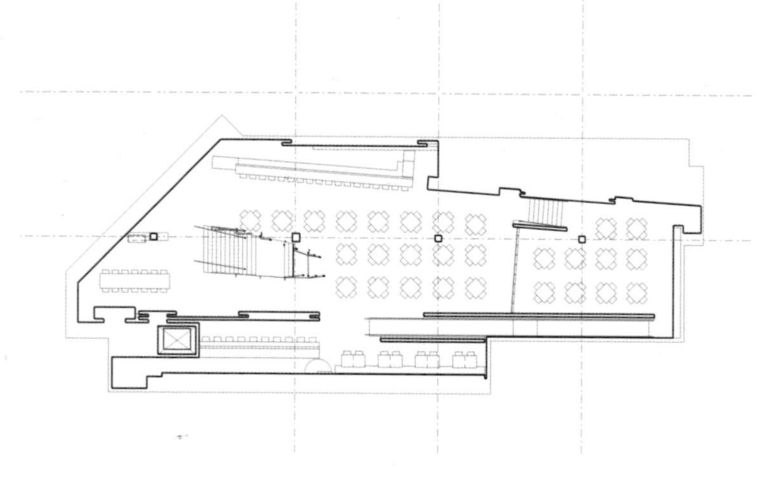

Ground floor plan

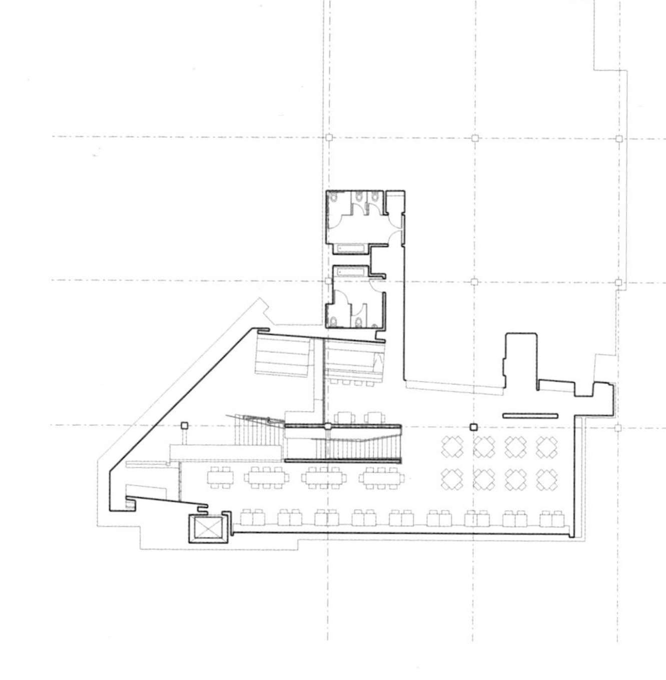

Second floor plan

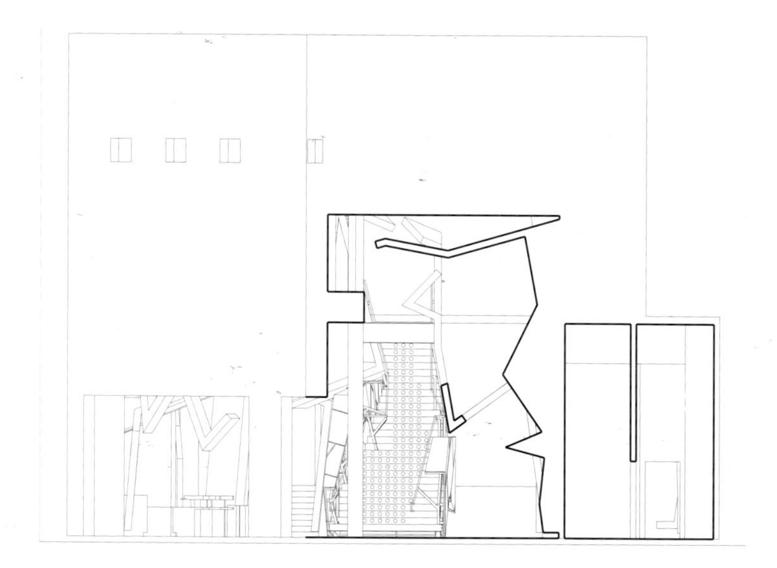

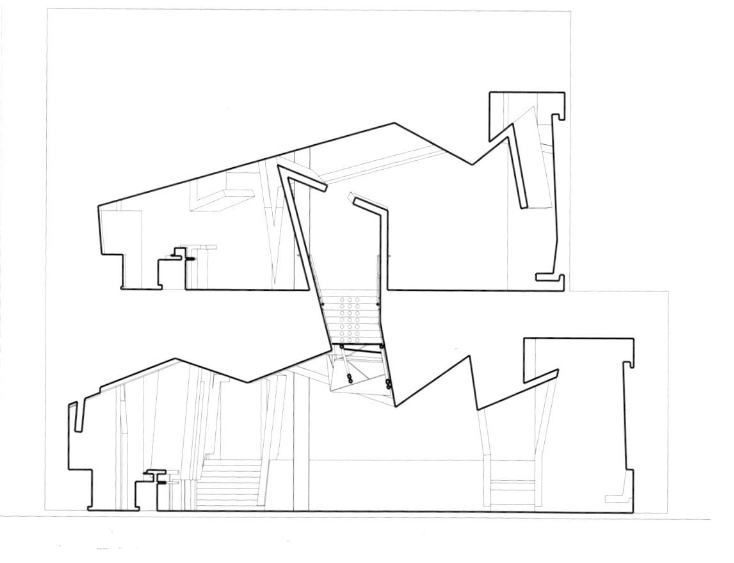

Sections

Lutèce

Morphosis | **Las Vegas**

The design for Lutèce, located in the heart of Las Vegas's casino district, revolved around incorporating all the intriguing elements that allude to the chaotic environment surrounding the restaurant. In this way, the architect aspired to create an oasis that avoids the frenzied strategic patterns of most of the city's eating establishments.

After passing through a small door inspired by Alice in Wonderland, the visitor leaves the chaos to arrive in a serene refuge that is defined by an interesting articulation of materials. References to the casino's complexity are not prohibited; rather, they are interpreted in a different way to create a new kind of relationship between the space and the visitor.

The formal language that the architects applied came from the abstraction of the classic formal dining room. The primary inspirations were the crystal chandelier above the central space and the fluidity produced between the zones of the restaurant and the bar. A bronze wall in the form of an elliptical cone wraps around the dining room, functioning as a gesture that organizes the general space. A glass surface around this piece both connects and divides the restaurant from the bar and the entrance.

The main inspirations of this restaurant are the original elements of a classic salon-dining room together with references to the formal chaos of Las Vegas casinos

This central piece is influenced by other elements, including a large format wall supporting bottles of wine that create should be interesting plays of light and shadow. This enormous cave transforms into an indirect lamp that defines the character of the bar and grants access to the restaurant.

Architect: Morphosis

Photographer: Farshid Assassi

Address: 3355 S. Las Vegas Boulevard, Las Vegas, Nevada, USA

Opening date: November 1999

Surface area: 2,537 sq. feet

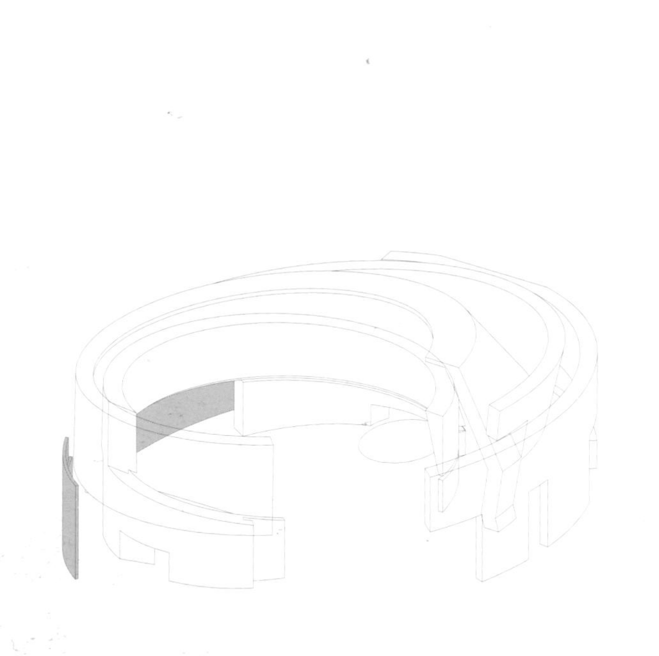

3D model

Ground floor plan

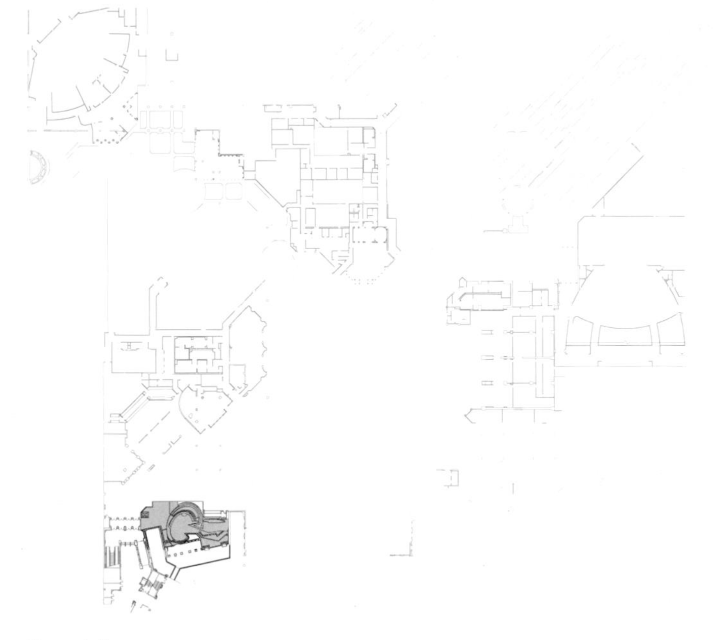

General plan

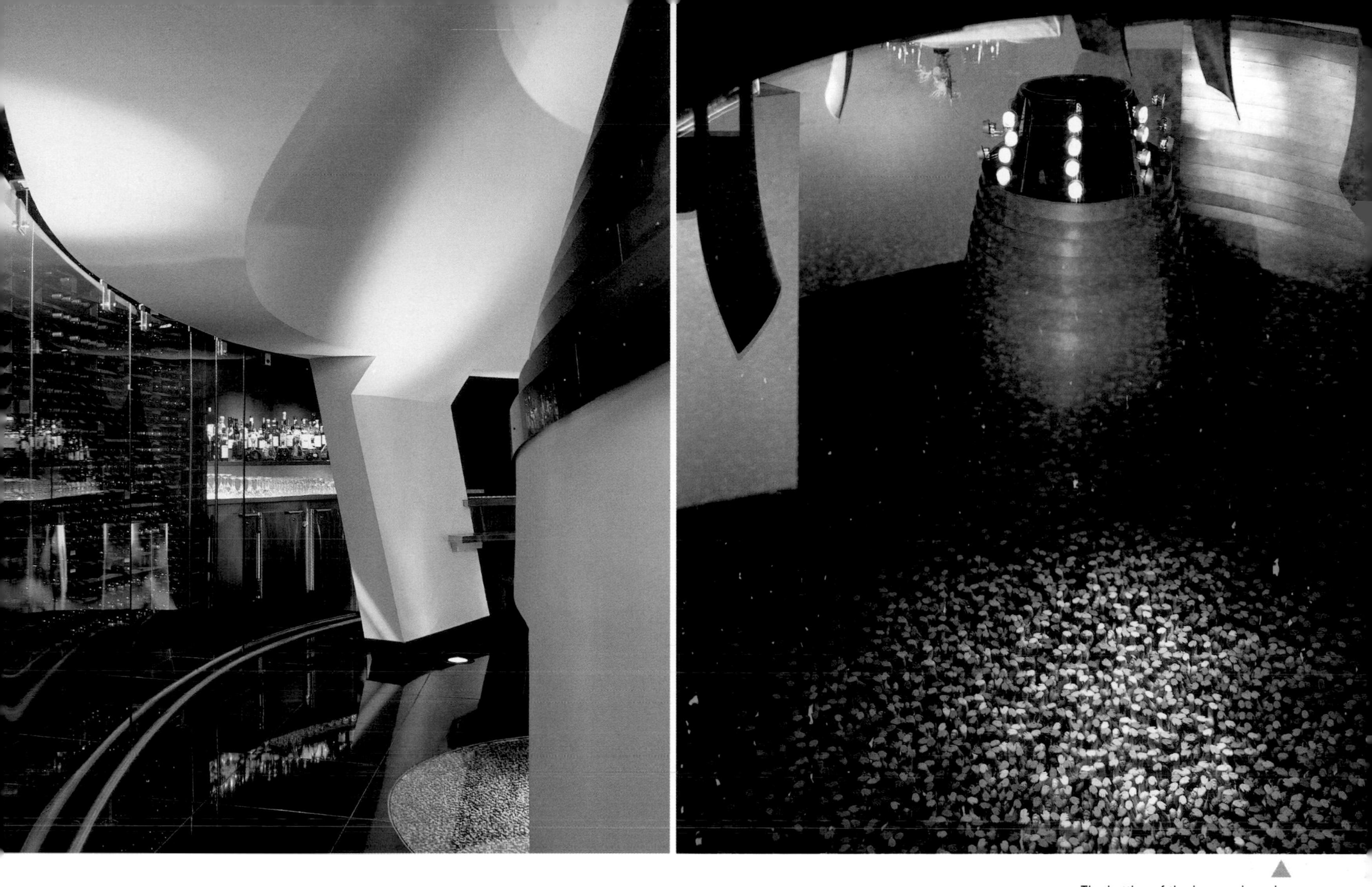

The bottles of the impressive wine collection create a play of reflections, textures, and light and shadow that evokes a special ambience within the restaurant.

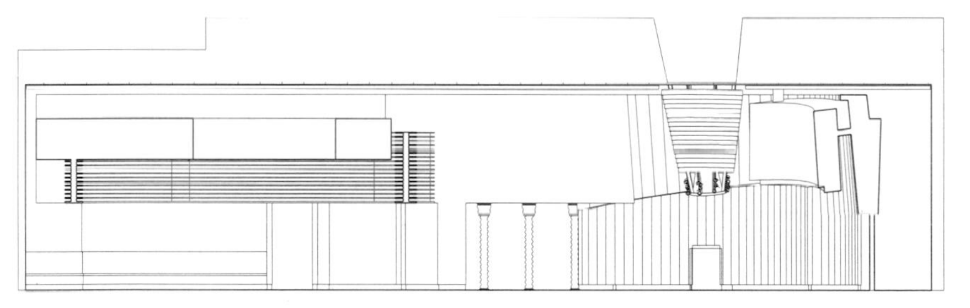

Longitudinal section

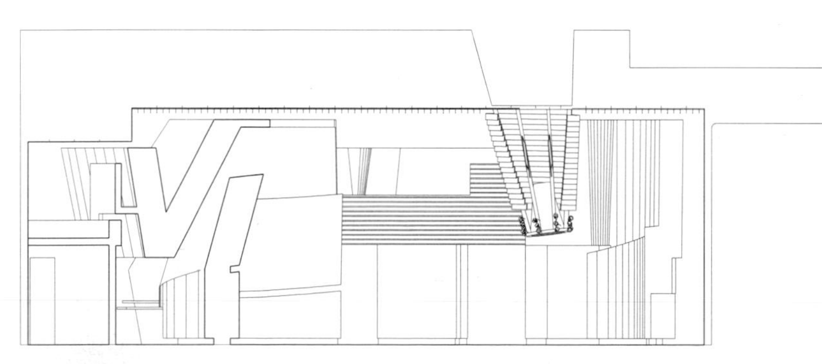

Transversal section

Shi Bui

Susana Ocaña, Paraservis | **Barcelona**

The architects´s assignment consisted in creating a Japanese restaurant with contemporary and austere undertones. The idea was to avoid overusing the typical traditional elements found in Japanese restaurants, and to design a subtle yet comfortable atmosphere based on the Asian philosophy. The restaurant stretches out over two floors with a minimum height that are linked by a courtyard. One of the floors is located under the gradient of the street where there is no natural light.

To achieve the project's goal, the architects analyzed the spatial configuration and opted for an approach based on three premises: texture of the materials, uniform chromaticism, and control of light. These elements resolved the connection between the two floors in two ways: by converting the courtyard into a Japanese garden and by creating important visual openings linked by color and light. The staircase is the key connection between the two floors. Both functional and formal, it captures the visitor's attention using a sequence of full and empty spaces, and light and shadow.

As a point of reference in the design of the restaurant, the architects paid heed to the literal translation of the restaurant's name which means "know when to stop"

Shi Bui was conceived as a cardboard box inside another box. The principal materials —paper and wood — pay tribute to the Japanese culture. Small vegetative and literary images liven up the atmosphere. To complete the box and to chromatically balance the space as a whole, the architects hung a series of quadrangular panels that serve as aesthetic screens and that hide certain technical installations.

Architect: Susana Ocaña, Paraservis

Photographer: Eugeni Pons

Address: Comte d'Urgell 272, Barcelona, Spain

Opening date: September 2000

Surface area: 4,430 sq. feet

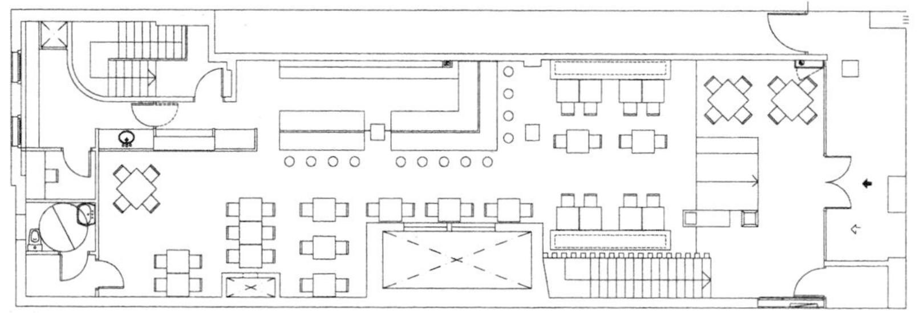

Basement floor

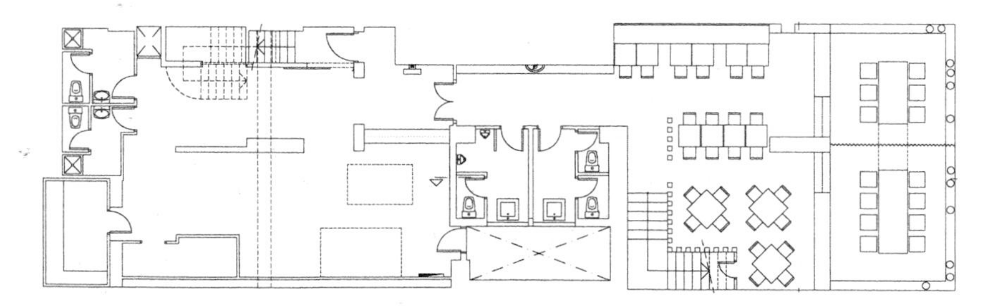

First floor

Diners can access the restaurant by way of a large glass surface that fuses the interior and exterior.

The furnishings are placed in the center of the space while the walls remain free of any element that might distort its clean and austere surface.

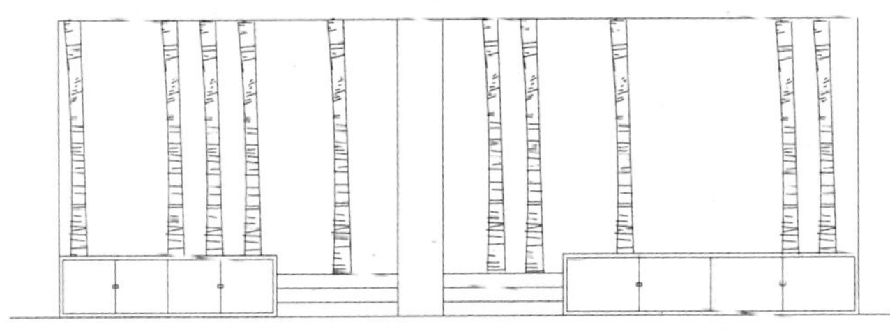

Transversal section

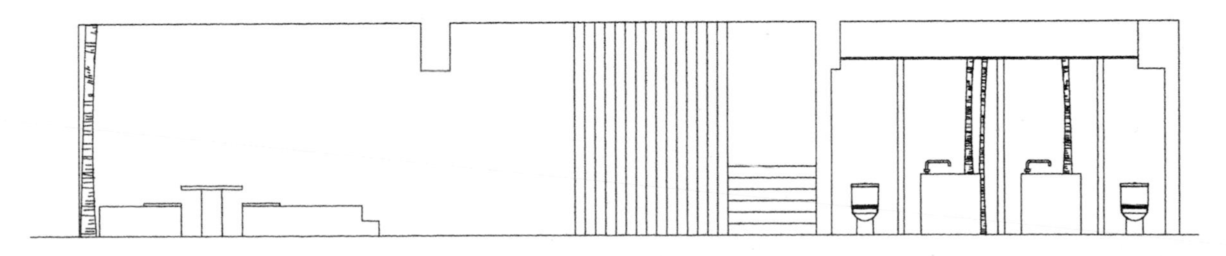

Longitudinal section

The succession of full and empty spaces formed by the staircase column makes it an important element that both links the two floors and that creates a play of chromaticity and light.

The bathrooms follow the same principles as the main space. The architects achieved a sense of diaphanous space by opening the bathroom onto the garden, which serves as an indirect source of light.

Central Snack

Heinz Lutter | **Vienna**

This restaurant is located on the first floor of a commercial center in Vienna, at the entrance to a cinema complex. The architectural concept was to arrange the space in two ways: a lateral structure organizes the functions of the restaurant's program, and in a vertical structure configures the formal elements.

The lateral arrangement includes the areas of the restaurant, the snack zone, and the bar. The snack area is directly connected to the commercial center and forms parts of its pedestrian activity. The restaurant is located in the back part in order to provide a more intimate atmosphere. The bar, situated in the middle of the two areas, is the element that unifies the entire space. Two large-format screens show videos and define the lateral structure.

The vertical organization is defined by the layout of the chairs and tables, th[illegible]e and information elements, the bar, the structural beams of the [illegible] ducts of the air conditioning system. The floor, the chairs, and the tables are made of wood of a similar color. The service elements and the bar are made of panels of perforated wood sheets that produce the effect of a lattice. The air conditioning ducts are painted gray, the same color as the false ceiling.

> The design pr[illegible]is restaurant crea[illegible]eful image through m[illegible] intervention and t[illegible] of few materials

The front façade of the establishment consists of large sliding doors, also made of perforated sheets. When the restaurant is open, the doors slide back to integrate the space with the exterior.

Architect: Heinz Lutter

Collaborators: Florian Röd

Photographer: Margherita Spiluttini

Address: Landstrasse/Haupstrasse 2a/2b, Vienna, Austria

Opening date: July 2000

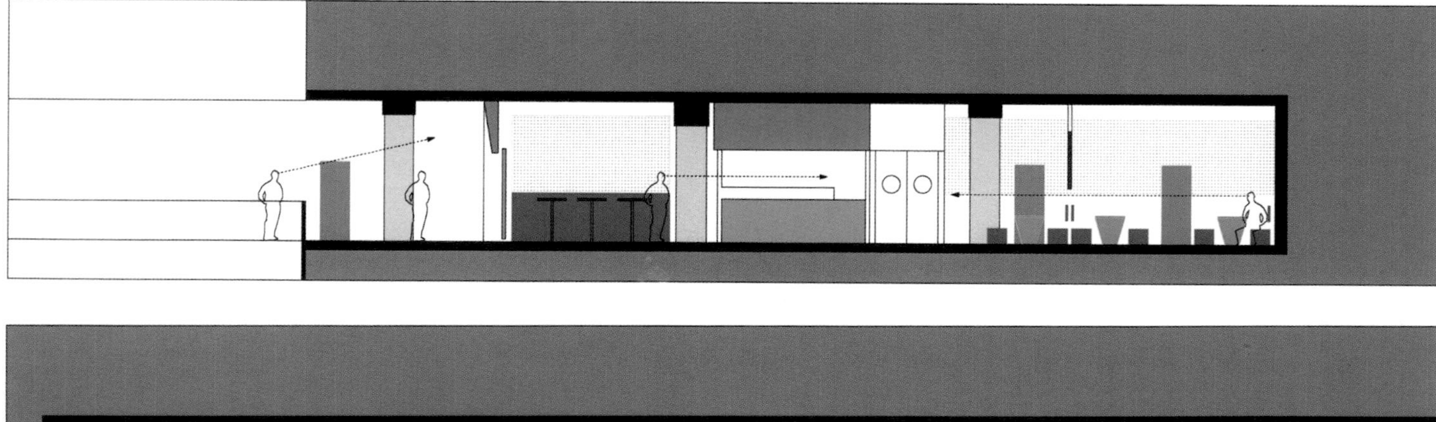

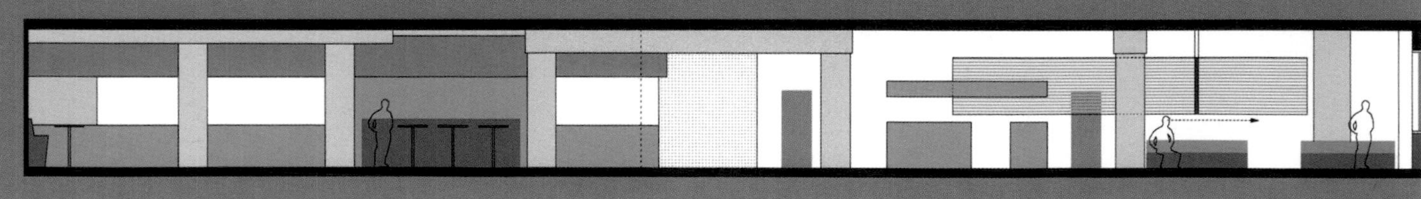

Sections

▲
The volumes of the space and the texture of the perforated wooden panels generate diverse transparencies and visual relations.

Lamps made of industrial cut glass are suspended from the false ceiling and used in all three areas to unify the space.

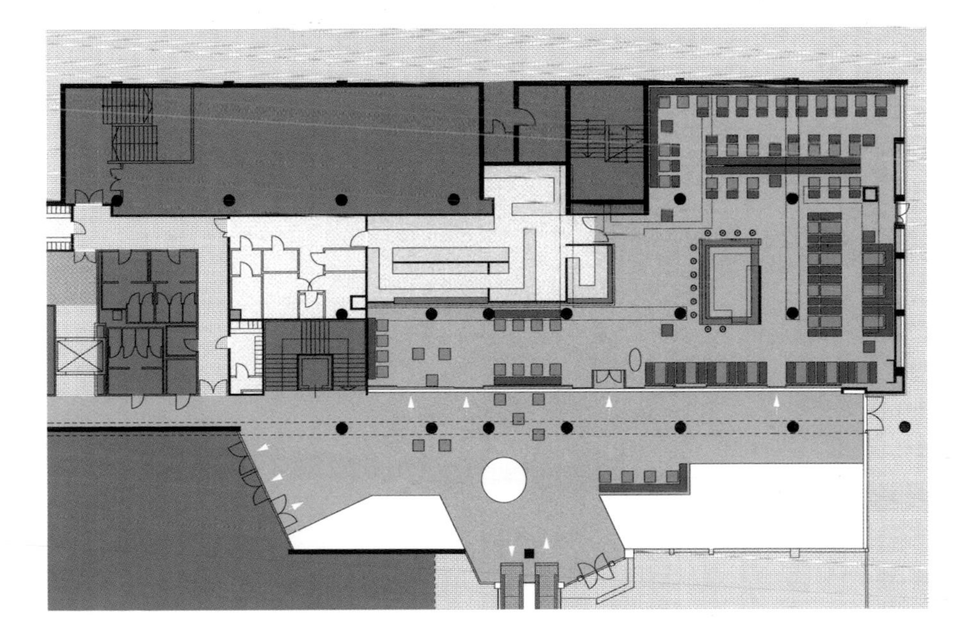

General plan

▲ The restaurant's existing structure served as the element of composition in the interior design. To the eye, the columns appear as separate objects in the space, while the direction of the beams determines the layout of the furnishings and dividing panels.

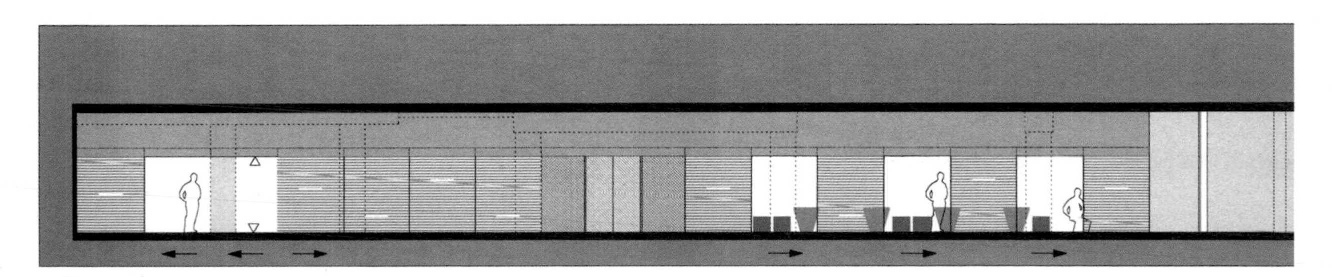

Section

The Brasserie

Diller & Scofidio | **New York**

The assignment awarded to Diller & Scofidio to remodel The Brasserie, a mythic restaurant in the Seagram building, was both an honor and a challenge. The Seagram building is one of the architectural paradigms of the Modern Movement. To achieve the contemporary and timeless spirit that skyscrapers exemplify, the project was carried out according to the principles — and challenges — of rationalism.

After dismantling the interior designed by architect Philip Johnson years ago, the original concrete surfaces were covered with new materials, such as wood, ceramics, terrazzo, or glass. To give this "second skin" special meaning, the new coverings serve certain structural or functional uses. Good examples are the ceiling made of strawberry tree wood and the floor of pear tree wood that doubles to create seats and vertical partitions that separate distinct atmospheres.

In tribute to the former The Brasserie, the architects preserved the descent from street level to the floor of the dining room and exaggerated it by adding a grand staircase with glass steps

Though the Seagram building was one of the first glass skyscrapers, the lower floor is curiously made out of stone and is opaque, without windows or views. This irony inspired the architects in several ways. In the entrance, they hung a large plasma monitor that shows the recordings of a video camera that films live scenes from the street. At the back of the dining room, a large glass screen covers the wall and reflects views of the restaurant. The glass also acts as a structural element in certain places by supporting seats.

Architects: Diller & Scofidio, Charles Renfro, and Deane Simpson

Collaborators: Ben Rubin (video), Alan Burden (structures), Richard Saber (lighting), Mary Bright (curtains), Douglas Cooper (installations)

Photographer: Michael Moran

Address: 100 East 53rd Street, New York, USA

Opening date: 2000

Surface area: 6,290 sq. feet

EXIT

The tables and the bar stools are made out of a translucent resin base held up by a steel structure. In addition, there are various types of chairs: some made of wood that hang from the ceiling and others made of resin or leather with metallic structures.

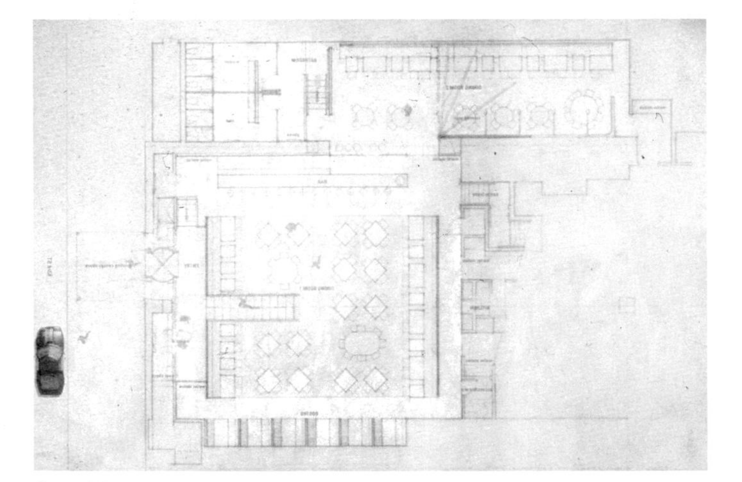

Ground floor

The architects compensated for the lack of windows by incorporating glass cloths that offer plays of transparency inside the restaurant. The use of monitors that show scenes from the street also avoids the feeling of isolation that could be provoked by the absence of windows.

A sensor in the entrance sets off a video camera every time a client enters. The recording is projected on the 15 screens situated above the bar. Each screen shows a different person, and as new people arrive, the images change.

▲
In one area of the restaurant, inclined concrete partitions divide the space into small zones that provide intimacy.

Detailed sections

Kosushi Restaurant

Arthur de Mattos Casas | **São Paulo**

The characteristics of this restaurant, located in a small three-story building, demanded a careful intervention that would make the most of the difficult spatial conditions. The idea was to construct a concrete box that could be seen from the exterior. Though the interior design showcases only a few elements, they are aesthetically forceful. By combining different materials, the project makes reference to both the traditional Japanese aesthetic and to a contemporary and avant-garde language.

The architect planned the distribution of the different zones to reinforce and make the most of the restaurant's characteristics. The service areas are concentrated on one side to emphasize the space's longitudinal proportions and to create a succession of atmospheres along the passageway of the dining room. The resulting ambiences are defined by the different textures of the flooring, the materials covering the walls, the lighting fixtures, and the arrangement of the furnishings. In one space, there is a loft with a tatame floor for intimate receptions with 20 people.

The richness of the interiors is achieved through only a few decorative elements that are both forceful and expressive.

For the interior decoration, the architect incorporated objects by recognized designers and pieces designed by the architectural team for the project. Francisco Almeida designed the three lamps with a metallic structure and a canvas lining that are suspended from the ceiling of the central space. The lamps are clearly inspired by works from the designer Isamu Nogushi. The architect of the project, Arthur de Mattos Casas, designed the black chairs and Charles Eames created the chairs of orange acrylic.

Architect: Arthur de Mattos Casas

Collaborators: Lorenz Acherman, Francisco de Almeida (lighting), and Gilberto Elkis (garden)

Photographer: Tuca Reinés

Address: Arthur Ramos Street, São Paulo, Brazil

Opening date: February 2001

Surface area: 2,612 sq. feet

The exterior appears cold and enigmatic, while the interior exudes a warm atmosphere thanks to the materials used.

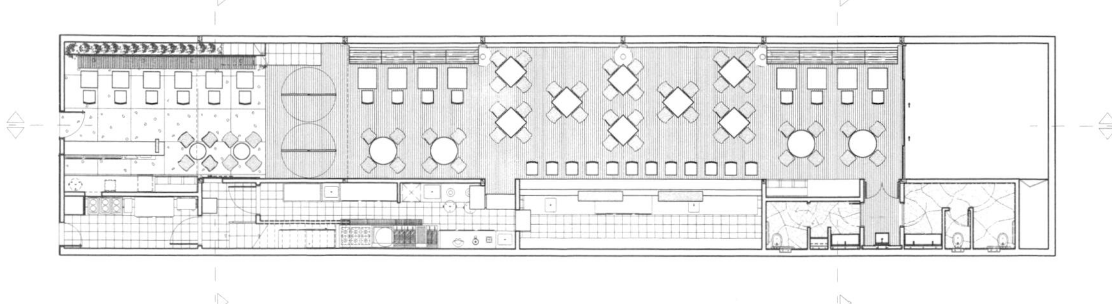

Plan

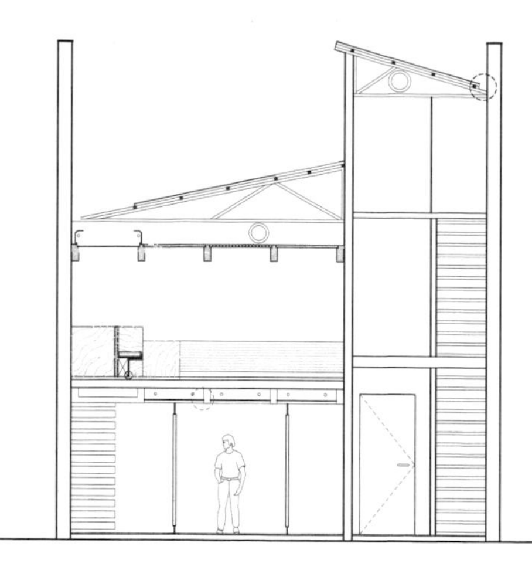

Transversal section

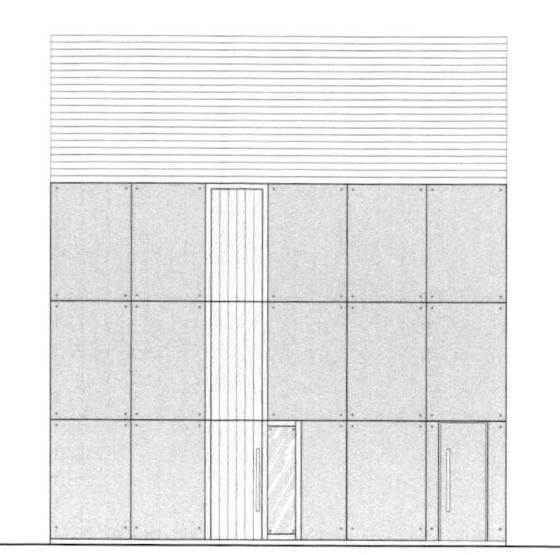

Façade

The lighting accentuates the different spatial conditions and plays with the composition of the furnishings.

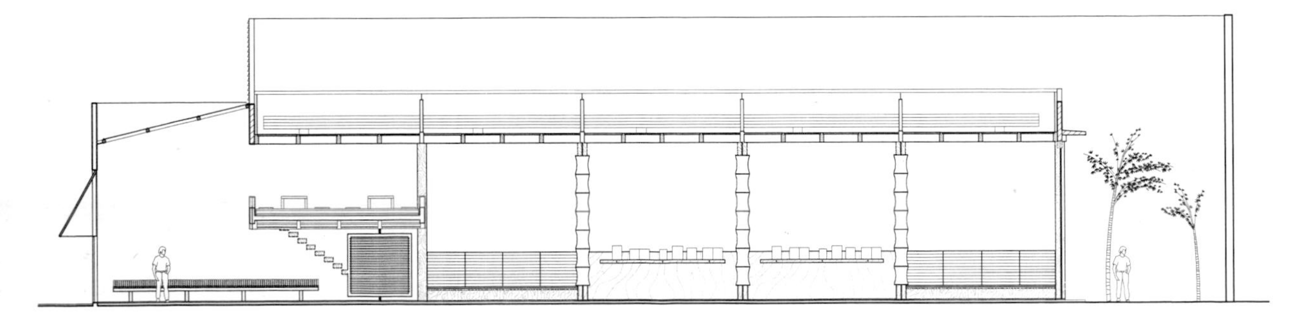

Longitudinal section

El Japonés

Sandra Teruella & Isabel López | **Barcelona**

This restaurant's basic idea came from a small restaurant located almost directly in front of it that was designed by the same architects. As with their previous project, the designers aimed to create an oriental aesthetic reinterpreted for the west. El Japonés avoids the characteristics of the typical Japanese restaurant and interprets the Japanese culture from a personal point of view. Influential factors include Japanese film, documentaries, works of art, and modern Japanese architecture.

The restaurant's façade alludes to the film "The Pillow Book" by Peter Greenway. Tall stalks of bamboo, planted in fashionable pots, surround the front door, which is covered with silver leaf. The designers conserved an existing pillar in the façade and created another of the same dimensions in order to establish symmetry, with the entrance in the middle. The two large openings on the sides were partially covered with brown rice, tucked in an air pocket between the glass, to avoid a view of the back of the benches placed against the windows.

The architects manipulated the materials in a forceful language, resulting in a space that interprets the contemporary Japanese aesthetic from a western point of view

Other references to the Japanese aesthetic include the use of straight forms to create a forceful yet austere atmosphere, the combination of cold and warm materials, and the contrast of colors and textures like matte and gloss. Red mosaic tiles are used inside the service areas. Reminiscent of Japanese lacquers, the tiles contrast with the sheets of zinc that cover the exterior of the bathrooms and the kitchen. Metallic mesh covers the 75 feet of the restaurant, providing privacy from the immediate neighbors and enriching the overall look of the space.

Architects: Sandra Teruella & Isabel López

Collaborators: Emma Masana and Virginia Angulo

Photographer: Eugeni Pons

Address: Pasaje de la Concepción 5, Barcelona, Spain

Opening date: 1999

Surface area: 3,655 sq. feet

EL J
APO
NÉS

◀
The restaurant has an informal and open character thanks to the use of solid, oiled wood for the floors, long benches, bartop, and community tables. Sheets of zinc used in the service zones and the application of silver leaf on the false ceiling also enrich the ambience.

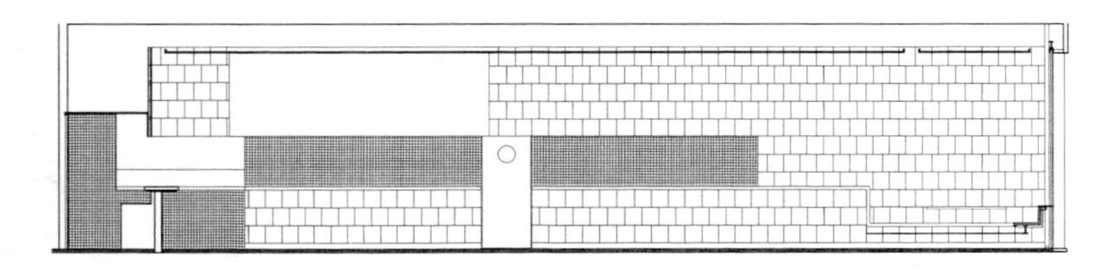

Interior plan

◀

The lighting had to respond to each of the utilities and to emphasize the features of the project. The designers used a xenon light in the pillars, close to the metallic covering, to play up their length. Over the two large tables near the façade, they hung Zettel´z lamps by designer Ingo Maurer. Pieces of paper hang from Maurer´s fixtures, reminiscent of those in Buddhist temples.

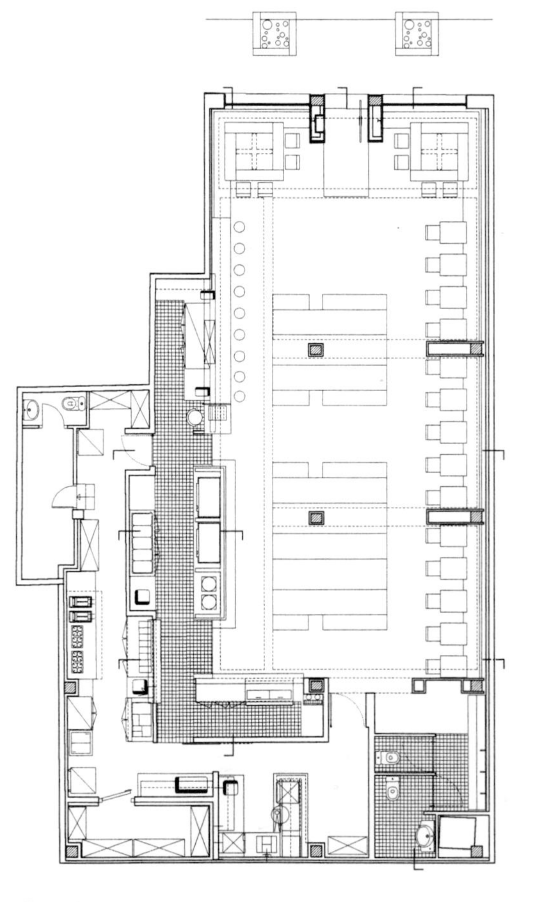

Floor plan

Souk

Guillermo Arias | Bogotá

The restaurant Souk is located in the La Candelaria neighborhood in the historic center of Bogotá. It reconciles all the recent transformations that the restaurant industry has experienced. The building conserved its two story colonial structure with adobe walls and mud tiles.

To resolve the space's narrow width, the project focused on the back of the building and on the restored colonial upper floor. The solution culminated in a narrow window that covers the upper part of the back wall, framing the dramatic Andean mountain range that borders the city.

To emphasize the space's depth, a bar was built into the left side of the first floor, using a striped composition of wood in two colors. On the other side, there is a staircase separated by a wall that is shorter than the ceiling and that reinforces the space's verticality and invites guests to cross the room. A dining room is situated on the upper floor, in the part of the house that conserves the original roof structure made of wood, cane, and mud tile. An iron bridge attached to the dining room leads to a terrace with views of the back part of the cathedral and the colonial barrio.

Basic materials and special details mixed with the building's original elements rescue and refresh the historic value of this colonial house

The architect used basic materials for the remodeling that create a dialogue with the house's original character yet give it a contemporary image. The smooth concrete walls and floors, as well as wood and iron, mix well with the existing elements.

Architect: Guillermo Arias

Photographer: Claudia Uribe/AXXIS

Address: Cra 6 Calle 10, Bogotá, Colombia

Opening date: May 2001

Surface area: 4,462 sq. feet

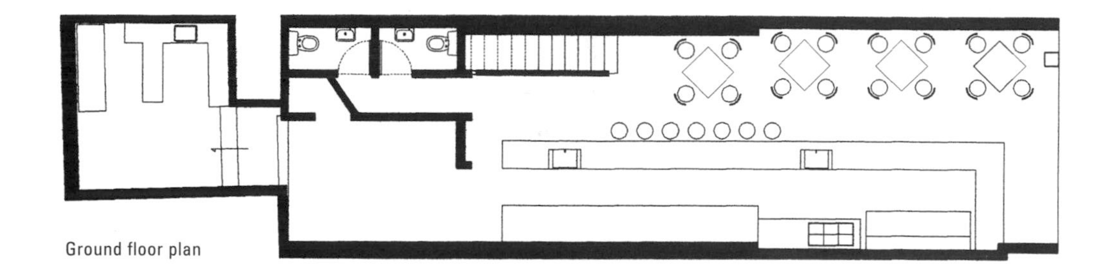

Ground floor plan

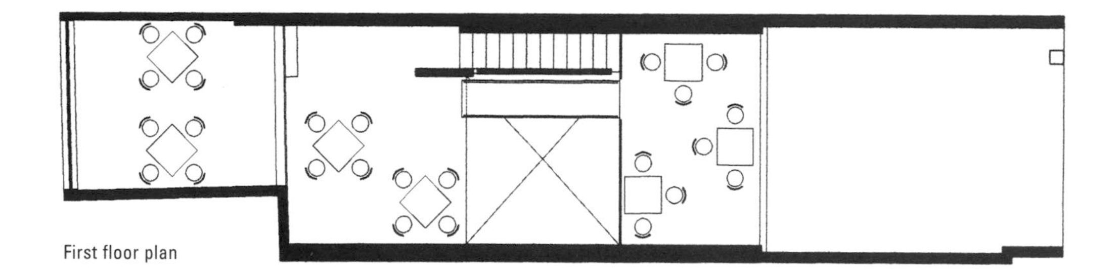

First floor plan

Indirect light bathes the walls and the ceiling while lamps, designed by the architect, are decorative elements that complement the interior ambience.

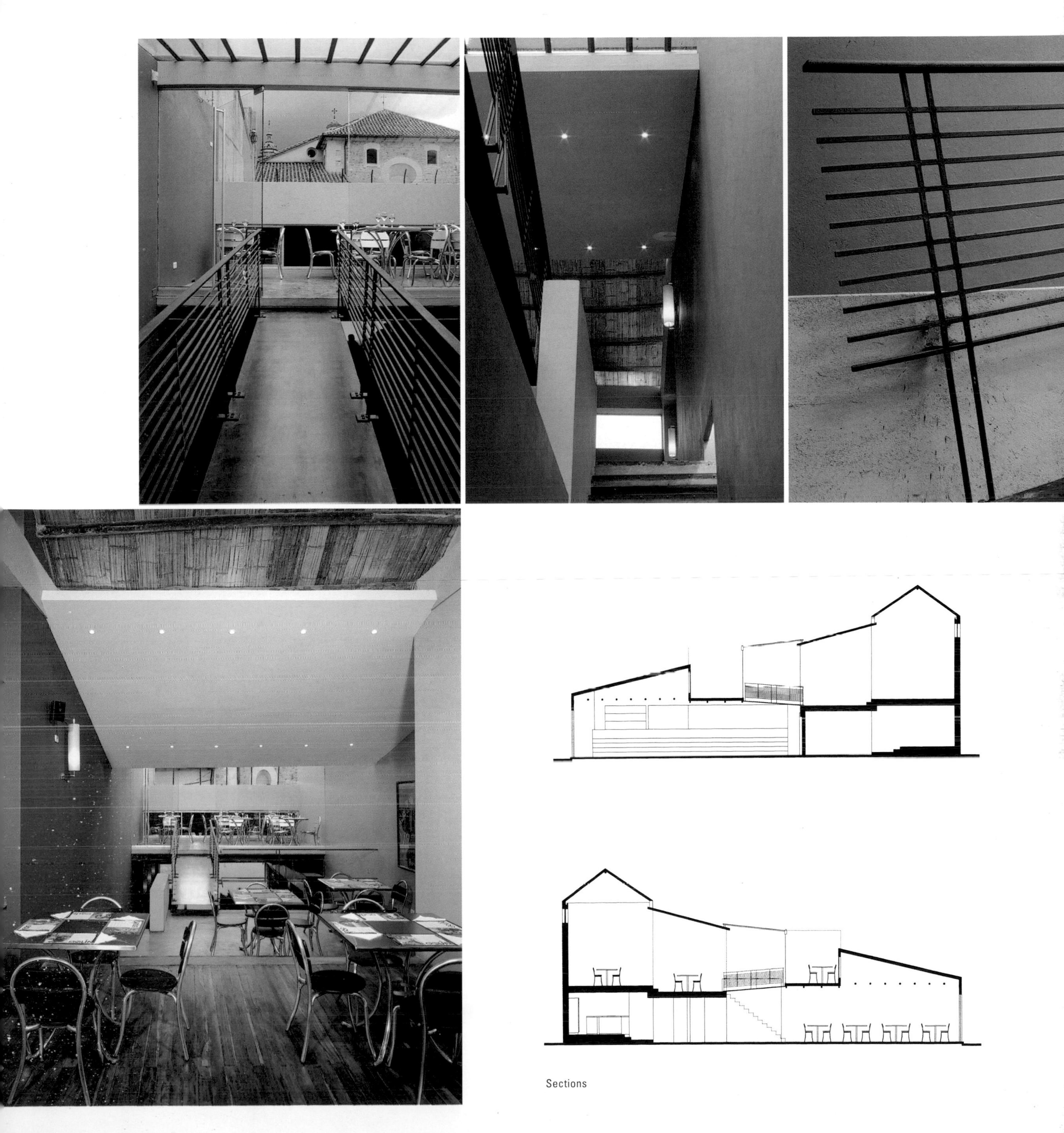

Sections

Bon

Philippe Starck | **Paris**

This project is the fruit of the interest of the client, Laurent Taieb, for high gastronomy, couple with his desire to create a place in which every corner is an antidote for the senses. The provocative space, located in an old, abandoned space in one of Paris's most exclusive neighborhoods, features design tricks and sumptuous decoration.

The prestigious designer Philippe Starck was entrusted to transform the interior and to bring it to the same level as similar restaurants. The project began with an interesting mix of elements with vast proportions. Thanks to the designer's theatrical flair, Chez Bon is like an ingenious set whose effects form part of the restaurant's spirit.

Chez Bon is made up of various ambiences, all connected, which adapt to the assortment of cuisines. The sushi bar, next to the entrance, defines the first space with its semicircular bar on which plates move on a mobile tray. On the other side, a long table the same height as the bar emphasizes the space's proportions. The tabletop is made of alabaster and the lighting situated under it establishes rich textures and a warm effect.

Theatricality, optical effects, and a varied mix of ambiences and gastronomic offerings define this elegant restaurant

The main room, connected to the exterior terrace at the back of the restaurant, is a space full of natural light and comfortable furnishings that invite lingering. The furniture includes soft sofas with white cotton cushions, tables covered with cloths, and chairs with a classic spirit. The large, orange-colored mirror creates the effect of a second continuous room and amplifies the setting's proportions.

Designer: Philippe Starck

Photographer: Mihail Moldoveanu

Address: Rue de la Pompe 25, Paris 16, France

Opening date: 2000

One of Chez Bon´s characteristics is the medley of ambiences. The settings range from the intimacy of a table inside a small space upholstered in canvas to the freshness of the exterior terrace, which is poised on a wooden platform and includes a simple garden.

The lighting effects emphasize the restaurant's theatricality and create different atmospheres. The alabaster tabletop reflects the light below it. Other resources that enrich the space are the projections of organic forms on classic frames and the lamps hung from the ceiling of the loft.